Bakary Diallo &

MW01005549

White War, Black Soldiers

Two African Accounts of World War I

Bakary Diallo & Lamine Senghor

White War, Black Soldiers

Two African Accounts of World War I

)(

Translated by
Nancy Erber and William Peniston

Edited, with an Introduction and Annotations, by
George Robb

Hackett Publishing Company, Inc.
Indianapolis/Cambridge

Copyright © 2021 by Hackett Publishing Company, Inc.

All rights reserved
Printed in the United States of America

24 23 22 21   1 2 3 4 5 6 7

For further information, please address
      Hackett Publishing Company, Inc.
      P.O. Box 44937
      Indianapolis, Indiana 46244-0937

      www.hackettpublishing.com

Cover design by E. L. Wilson
Interior design by Elana Rosenthal
Composition by Aptara, Inc.

Library of Congress Control Number: 2020943575

ISBN-13: 978-1-62466-952-1 (cloth)
ISBN-13: 978-1-62466-951-4 (pbk.)

The paper used in this publication meets the minimum requirements of American National Standard for Information Sciences—Permanence of Paper for Printed Library Materials, ANSI Z39.48–1984.

∞

Contents

Acknowledgments

This book project has been a few years in the making, and the editor and translators would like to thank the many people who have helped us along the way. First, and foremost, we are indebted to Rick Todhunter at Hackett Publishing for his unswerving support and patience. The two anonymous reviewers for Hackett provided numerous valuable suggestions from which the book has benefited. Bonnie Smith's enthusiasm for this project early on helped sustain us, and her advice was crucial in keeping us going. Christa Clarke and Molly O'Donnell provided valuable referrals regarding African history and culture. Delia Dunlap and Oumar Ba were especially helpful in clarifying many aspects of West African culture and languages. Lastly, Antoinette Burton and Ellen Ross read sections of this book in draft form and offered astute suggestions for revisions. To all these people, who generously gave their time and expertise, we express our gratitude.

Bakary Diallo in France in 1928, shortly before his return to Senegal. From Dorothy S. Blair, African Literature in French: A History of Creative Writing in French from West and Equatorial Africa *(Cambridge: Cambridge University Press, 1976). Reproduced with permission of The Licensor through PLSclear.*

Introduction

Strength and Goodness (*Force-Bonté*) by Bakary Diallo is one of the only memoirs of World War I ever written or published by an African. It remains a pioneering work of African literature as well as a unique and invaluable historical document about colonialism and Africa's role in the Great War. The book recounts in very personal terms Diallo's childhood in rural Senegal, his recruitment into the French Army of West Africa, and his combat experiences in Morocco and later in France, where he was seriously wounded at the Battle of the Marne in 1914. Diallo shares his first impressions of France and the French people, his relations with other African soldiers from different ethnicities and social ranks, his war experience as the leader of a segregated squad, and, after his injury, his interactions with the military bureaucracy and an informal support system of French civilians. Interspersed among Diallo's wartime recollections are his eloquent pleas for racial equality and the brotherhood of all nations. More controversially, Diallo also praises France's "civilizing mission" in Africa.

Lamine Senghor's *The Rape of a Country* (*La Violation d'un pays*) is another pioneering French work by a Senegalese veteran of World War I, but one that offers a stark contrast to *Strength and Goodness*. Senghor's short story is a dystopian fable about the evils of French imperialism and the exploitative nature of the Great War. Senghor wrote *The Rape of a Country* as a propaganda pamphlet for the Communist Party, and he hoped that his work would incite rebellion against French colonial rule in Africa.

Diallo's memoir was much celebrated as the first book in French by a black African author upon its publication in 1926, and it complemented the many war books written by European and American veterans at this time, such as Erich Maria Remarque's *All Quiet on the Western Front* (1929), Robert Graves's *Good-bye to All That* (1929), and Ernest Hemingway's *A Farewell to Arms* (1929). Unfortunately, *Strength and Goodness* has been out of print for decades and no English translation has ever been published. Senghor's *The Rape of a Country* never circulated widely at the time of its publication, and the French

1

Lamine Senghor in 1927, speaking at the League against Imperialism in Brussels.

government prevented its export to Africa. Although a new French language edition recently has been published, the work has still never been translated into English.

The centennial of World War I is an ideal moment to present *Strength and Goodness* and *The Rape of a Country* to a wider, English-reading public. Until recently, Africa's role in the war has been neglected by historians and largely forgotten by the general public. Eurocentric versions of the war still predominate in popular culture, including Peter Jackson's recent compilation of wartime film footage, *They Shall Not Grow Old* (2018), which includes no images of colonial troops.[1] Many historians, however, now insist that African participation in the 1914–1918 war is a large part of what made that conflict a *world* war. Significant fighting took place in Africa, and the continent's colonial

---

1. For a critique of Peter Jackson's "whitewashing" of the war, see Santanu Das, "Colors of the Past: Archive, Art, and Amnesia in a Digital Age," *American Historical Review* 124, no. 5 (December 2019): 1771–81.

rulers expropriated such vast quantities of raw materials, workers, and soldiers to sustain the war that they left chaos and famine in their wake. More than two million Africans served in World War I as laborers and soldiers, with some 10 percent of them dying. Bakary Diallo and Lamine Senghor were among the 140,000 West African soldiers who fought for France on the western front from 1914 to 1918. Almost 30,000 of these young men died for their colonial masters.[2]

Even as historians are reintegrating Africa into narratives of the Great War, they struggle to include African voices. Most African soldiers were drawn from rural, nonliterate backgrounds and few firsthand accounts of the war by Africans have survived. Some historians have begun recovering the lost voices of African soldiers through letters and oral histories. During the 1980s, Joe Lunn interviewed dozens of surviving African veterans of World War I as the basis for his 1999 book, *Memoirs of the Maelstrom: A Senegalese Oral History of the First World War.* In 1985, another researcher, Guy Thilmans, found a cache of letters written during World War I by four Senegalese soldiers stationed in France to a friend of theirs back home. A collection of these letters was published in 2014.[3] Given the scarcity of firsthand accounts of the war by Africans, *Strength and Goodness* is a pivotal addition to our knowledge of the war. While over one thousand European, North American, and Australian soldiers published memoirs about World War I, only one African, Bakary Diallo, did so.

Diallo was an unlikely chronicler of the war, as he was illiterate when he first joined the military. Born in 1892 in M'Bala in the Futa Toro region of northwest Senegal, Bakary Diallo spent his childhood as a shepherd among the Fula people. Dissatisfied with his monotonous pastoral life, he left his village for the city of Saint-Louis, where he joined the French Colonial Army on February 4,

---

2. Richard S. Fogarty, *Race and War in France: Colonial Subjects in the French Army, 1914–1918* (Baltimore: Johns Hopkins University Press, 2008), 27.

3. For examples of African voices from World War I, see Joe Lunn, *Memoirs of the Maelstrom: A Senegalese Oral History of the First World War* (Portsmouth, NH: Heinemann, 1999); Christian Koller, "Representing Otherness: African, Indian and European Soldiers' Letters and Memoirs," in *Race, Empire and First World War Writing*, ed. Santanu Das (Cambridge: Cambridge University Press, 2001), 127–42; Cyr and Francoise Descamps, Pierre Rosière, and Guy Thilmans, eds., *Tirailleurs Sénégalais: Témoignages épistolaires, 1914–1919* (Dakar: Éditions du Centaure, 2014); and Stephanie Newell, "An Introduction to the Writings of J.G. Mullen, An African Clerk in the *Gold Coast Leader*, 1916–19," *Africa* 78 (August 2008), 384–400.

1911. After a whirlwind training session with a diverse group of African recruits, Diallo and his comrades were sent to Morocco in May 1911 to suppress an Arab rebellion against French rule. When World War I broke out in August 1914, Diallo's unit was rushed to France, where it participated in the Battle of the Marne, halting the German advance on Paris. Having been promoted to corporal, Diallo volunteered to lead a night patrol of twelve men in a forest held by the Germans. He was seriously wounded on November 3, 1914, his jaw shattered by German gunfire. Bakary Diallo spent the next several years in a series of military hospitals and rest homes, where he endured thirteen separate operations to reconstruct his face. Awarded military honors, Diallo was able to obtain French citizenship in 1920, but he quit the army that same year, when the authorities refused to grant him equal pay with French soldiers. He remained in France for several years, working a series of menial jobs, including as doorman of the Hotel National in Monte Carlo. During these years of hardship, he was befriended and assisted by a number of French people, including the artist Lucie Cousturier, who helped him publish his memoirs, *Strength and Goodness*, in 1926. When he finally returned to Senegal in 1928, Bakary Diallo worked for the French colonial government as a messenger, interpreter, and finally, *chef de canton*. In 1953, he retired to his native village where he died in 1979 at age eighty-seven. Before his death, the French government awarded him the Légion d'honneur (Legion of Honor) for his service to the state.[4]

The Great War also plucked Lamine Senghor out of obscurity and led to his radicalization. An ethnic Serer, Senghor was born in 1889 into a family of peasant farmers near the coastal town of Joal, southeast of Dakar.[5] Like Diallo, he sought new opportunities, moving to Dakar in 1912, where he found employment as a clerk in the French petroleum company Maurel et Prom. During World War I, Senghor was drafted into the Colonial Army and served in the 68th Battalion of the *Tirailleurs Sénégalais* from 1916 to 1919. He experienced fierce combat at the Battle of the Somme and at Nivelle, where he was wounded. In 1917, he suffered a mustard gas attack near Verdun, permanently injuring his lungs. The army promoted Senghor

---

4. For biographical information on Bakary Diallo, see Mohamadou Kane, introduction to *Force-Bonté* (Paris: Nouvelles Éditions Africaines, 1985).

5. The Serer are the third largest ethnic group in Senegal, after the Wolof and Fula.

to sergeant and awarded him the Croix de Guerre. Like Diallo, he was granted French citizenship for his military service. After the war, Senghor married a French woman, Eugénie Comont, and worked as a postman in Paris.[6]

Unlike Bakary Diallo, Lamine Senghor rejected France's "civilizing mission" as a sham, and he denounced the war as an imperialist struggle in which Africans were used as cannon fodder. Senghor joined the French Communist Party and, during the 1920s, became one of the leading African spokesmen against colonialism. In 1927, he published *The Rape of a Country*, a propaganda pamphlet that condemned both French imperialism and the Great War. Later that year, Senghor died of lung disease related to his wartime injuries. He was only thirty-eight years old.

Colonial Soldiers in the Service of Empire

The vast maritime empires of the nineteenth century would not have been possible without the countless "native" troops who enforced European authority. Diallo's enlistment in the *Tirailleurs Sénégalais*, or Senegalese Riflemen, was part of a long tradition of colonized people joining the armies of their European rulers. Since the eighteenth century, imperial powers like France and Great Britain maintained vast armies of local soldiers in their overseas colonies. British forces in India and French in Africa contained hundreds of thousands of native soldiers who were commanded by a small body of white officers. These colonial soldiers conquered additional territories for the Europeans and helped maintain imperial rule over their fellow Africans and Asians.[7]

That so many subject peoples were willing to participate in their own domination testifies to the complexity of imperial politics. Some men

6. For details of Lamine Senghor's life, see introduction to Lamine Senghor, *La Violation d'un pays et autres écrits anticolonialistes*, ed. David Murphy (Paris: L'Harmattan, 2012), xix–xxi.

7. On the use of "native" troops by European colonial powers, see David Killingray and David Omissi, eds., *Guardians of Empire: The Armed Forces of the Colonial Powers, c. 1700–1964* (Manchester: Manchester University Press, 1999); Ronald Lamothe, *Slaves of Fortune: Sudanese Soldiers and the River War* (Woodbridge, UK: James Currey Press, 2011); and Timothy Stapleton, *African Police and Soldiers in Colonial Zimbabwe* (Rochester, NY: University of Rochester Press, 2011).

who joined colonial armies came from peoples with a strong martial tradition, like Sikhs in British India, and they saw their military service for Europeans as a way to uphold this tradition and to prove their manhood. Others became colonial soldiers in search of adventure or because these positions conferred status and were comparatively well paid, with the promise of a pension following years of service. After generations of imperial rule, some Africans and Asians simply accepted European power as a fact of life, deciding that "if you can't beat them, join them." People tried to make the best of their circumstances while living under a repressive colonial regime.

Colonial authorities were also savvy in their use of indigenous troops, seldom stationing these men in areas where they knew the local people. The British and French Empires were racially and ethnically diverse, and the authorities often used soldiers from one ethnic group to police another. For example, the British might use Muslim soldiers from the north of India to suppress riots by Hindus in the south of the country. Bakary Diallo himself was part of the *Tirailleurs Sénégalais*, a French West African force used against an Arab revolt in North Africa.

The French government created the *Tirailleurs Sénégalais* in 1857 to defend its then small empire in West Africa. At first drawn largely from Senegal, the force played a key role in conquering vast territories that would become the colonial federations of French West Africa and French Equatorial Africa. Over time, soldiers for the *Tirailleurs Sénégalais* would be drawn from across sub-Saharan Africa, especially from modern-day Mali and Burkina Faso, but they all would continue to be called Senegalese. In the early twentieth century, France began using this West African army as an expeditionary force in other parts of its empire, most notably to suppress a rebellion in Morocco, an episode described in great detail in *Strength and Goodness*. As it turned out, the Moroccan campaign proved to be a dress rehearsal for the deployment of African soldiers to France during World War I.[8]

The French imagined that their African soldiers would help spread loyalty to the mother country throughout the continent. Some colonial soldiers, like Bakary Diallo, came to identify with the "civilizing

---

8. For the origins of France's use of African soldiers, see Sarah Davis Westwood, "*Ceddo, Sòfa, Tirailleur:* Slave Status and Military Identity in Nineteenth-Century Senegambia," *Slavery and Abolition* 39, no. 3 (2018): 518–39; and Myron Echenberg, *Colonial Conscripts: The Tirailleurs Sénégalais in French West Africa, 1857–1960* (Portsmouth, NH: Heinemann, 1991), 19–27.

mission" of the French Empire, though others saw their service in more professional terms. However much French officials might idealize the role of the *Tirailleurs Sénégalais*, the bottom line was that it was far more economic to employ indigenous troops than to bring in Europeans. Training, equipping, and paying African soldiers cost half the price of utilizing French soldiers. The use of African soldiers also spared Europeans from the catastrophic effects of tropical diseases. For example, during the French conquest of Madagascar in 1895, only twenty-five French soldiers died in combat, compared to six thousand who succumbed to disease, mostly malaria.[9]

Imperial recruiting practices were also influenced by nineteenth-century race theory which posited that certain non-European peoples were more naturally warlike (and masculine) than others who were more servile (and feminine). Colonial armies drew more heavily upon the former. In British India, for example, the army recruited almost exclusively among Sikhs and Muslims in the Punjab, whom it viewed as fierce and brave, rather than Hindus, whom it derided as weak and effeminate. Likewise, the French divided their subject peoples into *races guerrières* (warrior races) and *races non-guerrières* (non-warrior races). In North Africa, they admired the Moroccans as a savage, warlike people and derided the Tunisians as womanly. West Africans were believed to be the most warlike of all France's colonial peoples, but within the vast territory of French West Africa, some ethnic groups, like the Fula and Bambara, were deemed warrior races, while others, like the Susu, were only thought suitable for porterage and other manual labor.[10]

Although the French lauded West Africans as "natural soldiers," they primarily saw them as followers rather than as leaders. In the racist formulation of the era, Africans were fierce and brave but also childlike and dependent. They supposedly lacked the intelligence necessary for taking the initiative, needing the guidance of European officers. Despite the French Republic's commitment to meritocracy

---

9. Fogarty, *Race and War in France*, 19.

10. Joe Lunn, "*Les Races Guerrières*: Racial Preconceptions in the French Military about West African Soldiers during the First World War," *Journal of Contemporary History* 34, no. 4 (1999): 517–36. For other examples of "martial race" policy in Africa, see Timothy Parsons, "'Wakamba Warriors Are Soldiers of the Queen': The Evolution of the Kamba as a Martial Race," *Ethnohistory* 46, no. 4 (1999): 671–701; and Myles Osborne, "Controlling Development: 'Martial Race' and Empire in Kenya, 1945–59," *Journal of Imperial and Commonwealth History* 42, no. 3 (2014): 464–85.

and careers open to talent, maintaining colonial racial hierarchies was
more important than providing genuine opportunities for Africans to
advance through the ranks. Black soldiers could only hope to become
noncommissioned officers (NCOs), like corporals or sergeants. Only
a handful ever reached higher grades as lieutenants or captains.[11]
However, the Colonial Army relied heavily on African NCOs, like
Bakary Diallo, to train new recruits and enforce discipline. Known as
grades indigènes (native ranks), colonial NCOs acted as intermediaries
and translators between French officers and African soldiers. It was
seen as important for officers to pick talented men for this role and
to ensure that they learned better French.[12] Diallo's promotion to
corporal helped ensure his postwar career in the colonial service.

Communication within France's Colonial Army proved a serious
problem, as West African recruits spoke dozens of different languages,
and the French, even after decades of colonial rule, had made little
effort to establish schools or promote literacy. In 1913, on the eve of
World War I, less than 1 percent of children in French West Africa
were enrolled in French schools. The practical difficulties in teaching
large numbers of illiterate conscripts to speak French led the military
to develop a simplified, or "pidgin," French, which was known as *petit
nègre*. Diallo gives examples of the French lessons he and his fellow
conscripts received. When French people heard colonial soldiers speak
this "baby French," it only reinforced racist ideas that Africans were
childlike. Bakary Diallo's eventual mastery of proper French set him
apart from most African soldiers who only spoke the pidgin variety.[13]

Another distinctive practice within the French Colonial Army was
allowing African soldiers to bring their wives and children along with
them on campaigns. This privilege was seen as an important recruiting
tool and was thought to prevent homesickness. The French referred to
the soldiers' camp followers as *la smala*, an expression adopted from
Arabic, meaning "entourage." Diallo gives an extensive description of

11. Werner Glinga, "*Le tirailleur sénégalais:* A Protagonist of African Colonial
Society," in *Self-Assertion and Brokerage: Early Cultural Nationalism in West Africa*, ed.
P. F. de Moraes Farias and Karin Barber (Birmingham, UK: Centre for West African
Studies, 1990), 149.

12. Fogarty, *Race and War in France*, 112–14.

13. Fogarty, *Race and War in France*, 133–68. The French Army utilized a handbook
of "pidgin" French: *Le Français tel que le parlent nos tirailleurs sénégalais/French as it is
spoken by our Senegalese infantrymen* (Paris: L. Fournier, 1916).

these camp followers in *Strength and Goodness*. Unfortunately, African soldiers were not allowed to bring their families with them to France during World War I, as this was seen as too costly and disruptive.[14]

Bakary Diallo joined the French Colonial Army at the very moment when France began to see African soldiers as a vital adjunct to French power within Europe rather than as a home guard for Africa. Among the most forceful advocates of this view was Charles Mangin, a French officer who had served with the Colonial Army in Africa. For Mangin Africa represented an inexhaustible reservoir of soldiers to counteract France's falling birthrate and smaller population than her rival Germany. In the early twentieth century, France's population of forty million compared unfavorably to Germany's seventy million, but, as Mangin noted, the French *Empire* contained another one hundred million people on whom France could draw. (Germany's overseas empire was comparatively small.) Mangin supported the creation of a greatly enlarged African Army, which he labeled *la force noire* (the black force), for service in Europe or wherever it was needed.[15]

Initially, Mangin's scheme met with considerable opposition. Many military leaders believed that Africans were too backward to constitute a modern fighting force. Left-wing politicians, like Socialist Party leader Jean Jaurès, feared that African soldiers might be used to suppress strikes and labor activism in France. Frustrated by the French government's lack of support for his plan, Mangin appealed directly to the French people through a press campaign and with his best-selling book, *La Force noire* (1910).[16] Mangin's book was undergirded by racist ideas that Africans were naturally savage, but that their savagery easily could be harnessed in the service of France since they were also pliable and easily led. According to Mangin: "Black recruits learn by imitation and suggestion; they have done very little thinking before joining up, and one can tap into their subconscious almost without appealing first to their conscious minds." Above all, Mangin appealed to the idea

---

14. Sarah Zimmerman, "*Mesdames Tirailleurs* and Indirect Clients: West African Women and the French Colonial Army, 1908–1918," *International Journal of African Historical Studies* 44, no. 2 (2011): 299–322; and Gregory Mann, *Native Sons: West African Veterans and France in the Twentieth Century* (Durham, NC: Duke University Press, 2006), 151–53. Charles Mangin defends *la smala* in his influential book about African soldiers, *La Force noire/The Black Force* (Paris: Hachette, 1910), 292.

15. For a discussion of Mangin's influence, see Echenberg, *Colonial Conscripts*, 28–31.

16. Echenberg, *Colonial Conscripts*, 28; and Fogarty, *Race and War in France*, 21.

of an imperial France supported by a mighty black army. He boasted that the French Empire in Africa was "bigger than Europe itself and within fifty years will have one billion inhabitants."[17]

Government and Politics in French West Africa

While the Colonial Army in Africa grew in size and importance, the French governing apparatus remained small, even minimal. As Bakary Diallo made clear in his memoir, he never even saw a white person until he was a teenager. Although Senegal had been under French rule for two centuries, the French presence was small and mostly confined to coastal towns. In the African interior, the French ruled through local chiefs and village elders. Even though Diallo had little contact with Europeans before he joined the army, his fellow soldiers from coastal Senegal (like Lamine Senghor) would have been more familiar with colonial culture, and this would not have been a positive experience for most. European rule was a violent system that demanded constant deference. As summarized by historian Joe Lunn: "Africans were slapped at the slightest provocation, beaten for failing to remove their hats at the approach of European officials, whipped by malicious *commandants* for offenses such as impeding the movement of their horses, and offered derisory compensation when French negligence caused injury, such as the death of their children."[18]

Senegal was France's oldest colonial possession in West Africa, and its political administration was unique and more complicated than was the case in colonies established later. There were four coastal settlements in Senegal (Saint-Louis, Dakar, Gorée, and Rufisque) that enjoyed special status. Known as the Four Communes, these towns contained a sizeable proportion of French civil servants, army officers, and merchants, known as *colons*. Closely associated with the white *colons* was a mixed-race group of Euro-Africans known as *métis* or *creoles* who were French-speaking and often employed in clerical

---

17. Mangin, *La Force noire*, 236, 355. Translations by Nancy Erber.

18. Lunn, *Memoirs of the Maelstrom*, 16. For a more detailed discussion of colonial violence in French West Africa, see Alice L. Conklin, "Colonialism and Human Rights: A Contradiction in Terms? The Case of France and West Africa, 1895–1914," *American Historical Review* 103, no. 2 (1998): 419–42.

positions within the colonial administration. The African residents of the Four Communes were known as *originaires*, and, like the *métis*, gained certain political rights following the French Revolution of 1789: they could vote in municipal elections and could elect a deputy who represented the Communes in the French parliament, or Chamber of Deputies, in Paris. However, the *originaires* were subject to local Islamic law, rather than the French Civil Code, and if they moved beyond the borders of the Communes, they lost their voting rights.[19]

The rest of Senegal, like all of French West Africa, enjoyed no rights of self-government. Here, the French divided the colony into large districts, called *cercles* (circuits), under the rule of an appointed *commandant de cercle* (circuit commander). The *cercles* were further subdivided into *cantons* (districts) that were each administered by a *chef de canton* (district chief). These officials collected taxes, requisitioned labor to keep roads and other infrastructure repaired, and recruited soldiers for the army. At the apex of this colonial bureaucracy was the governor-general for all of French West Africa, who resided in Dakar and answered to the minister of colonies in Paris.[20]

Political power in Senegal's Four Communes had long been dominated by the French *colons* and the *métis*. In the early twentieth century, however, the African *originaires* began to organize politically and to demand recognition as French citizens. Their spokesman was Blaise Diagne, an ethnic Wolof from Gorée, born in 1872. He had attended engineering school in Marseilles and entered the colonial customs service, having scored highly on the civil service exam. Married to a white woman from France, Diagne challenged the colonial racial hierarchy personally as well as politically. Blaise Diagne and his followers argued that the French Republic's commitment to equality and universal rights should nullify the French Empire's racist practices. In 1914, Diagne ran for the position of deputy for the Communes, and, against great odds, he won the election.[21]

---

19. Charles John Balesi, *From Adversaries to Comrades-in-Arms: West Africans and the French Military, 1885–1918* (Waltham, MA: Crossroads, 1979), 79–80.

20. On the French government of West Africa, see Alice L. Conklin, *A Mission to Civilize: The Republican Ideas of Empire in France and West Africa* (Stanford, CA: Stanford University Press, 1997), 11–37.

21. Balesi, *From Adversaries to Comrades-in-Arms*, 80–81. For a more detailed discussion of Diagne's rise to power, see G. Wesley Johnson, *The Emergence of Black Politics in Senegal: The Struggle for Power in the Four Communes, 1900–1920* (Stanford, CA: Stanford University Press, 1971).

Diagne had only been a member of the French Chamber of Deputies for a few weeks when World War I began. The war strengthened his position as an African leader since France came to depend more heavily on colonial resources and manpower as the struggle against Germany continued. In 1916, in exchange for his support for the war, Diagne secured the full rights of French citizenship for Africans living in Senegal's Four Communes. Outside the Communes, other Senegalese began hoping that by working for French victory in the war, they too could enhance their status within the French Empire.[22]

World War I in Africa

World War I represented the last phase of the Scramble for Africa in which a handful of European nations had divided the continent among themselves during the late nineteenth century. In a 1915 article on the "African Roots of the War," the African American intellectual W. E. B. DuBois argued that Africa lay at the heart of the World War since colonial competition had fueled animosity between the great powers.[23] Fighting began in Africa as soon as it did in Europe. In the early stages of the war, the French and British seized all of Germany's African holdings. As the war dragged on for years at a great cost of lives and money, the Allies determined to keep the German colonies as a partial compensation for their war debt. France and England's ability to marshal the vast human and material resources of their empires gave them tremendous advantages over Germany. African raw materials, such as metals, rubber, jute, and palm oil, were sucked up by the war effort at phenomenal rates. They were often obtained by colonial administrators at fixed prices well below market rates. In African colonies the war increased taxation and decreased spending on public works and social welfare, never high to begin with.[24]

Europeans also recruited Africans as soldiers and laborers in unprecedented numbers. As historian Hew Strachan emphasizes,

---

22. Echenberg, *Colonial Conscripts*, 44–45.

23. W. E. B. DuBois, "The African Roots of the War," *Atlantic Monthly*, May 1915, 707–9.

24. For the history of World War I in Africa, see Hew Strachan, *The First World War in Africa* (Oxford: Oxford University Press, 2004); and Melvin E. Page, ed., *Africa and the First World War* (London: Palgrave, 1987).

"never before in the history of Africa had manpower been mobilized on such a scale."[25] In addition to the hundreds of thousands of Africans who fought in Europe and the Middle East, many thousands more served as soldiers, carriers, and laborers for the Europeans across Africa. On a continent with few paved roads or railways, more than a million African carriers transported weapons, food, and other supplies over thousands of miles of inhospitable terrain. They also cut roads, unloaded ships, and set up camps for French and British colonial forces. Officially, all those serving as carriers were volunteers, but in reality many were sent by chiefs or forcibly taken in quotas. "Carrier recruitment" was a euphemism for forced labor, and carriers often worked under conditions little better than slavery. They were overworked and underfed, their pay often in arrears, and, unlike soldiers, had no prospect of a pension or disability allowance. Their death rate was among the worst of all the war's participants, their bodies buried in mass, unmarked graves.[26]

France's extraction of raw materials, conscripts, and laborers from its African colonies exacerbated tensions within the empire and further alienated already disaffected elements in the population. Colonial soldiers' service to France engendered a greater sense of entitlement, while unequal treatment of these soldiers increased their resentment of empire. Likewise, France's authoritarian rule over its colonies proved difficult to reconcile with the claim that it was defending democracy and the rights of small nations like Belgium against German militarism.

German propaganda certainly delighted in pointing out that the defender of Belgium was the oppressor of Morocco and Madagascar. Indeed, the whole history of French imperial expansion could be seen as the conquest of the weak by the strong. Although the French Third Republic was a more open and democratic society than Imperial Germany, France's overseas colonies seldom benefited from its democratic traditions. German propaganda in neutral countries,

---

25. Strachan, *The First World War in Africa*, 3.

26. Geoffrey Hodges, *The Carrier Corps: Military Labor in the East African Campaign of 1914 to 1918* (New York: Greenwood Press, 1986). Death rates for carriers in Michèle Barrett, "Dehumanization and the War in East Africa," *Journal of War and Culture Studies* 10, no. 3 (2017): 238–52. Recently, the South African artist William Kentridge created a play, *The Head and the Load*, dramatizing the plight of African carriers during World War I. Jason Farago, "The African Toll of the Great War," *New York Times*, December 7, 2018.

like the United States, focused on the despotic nature of French imperialism, as well as the charge of betraying the white race through the use of African soldiers against Europeans. French (and British) reliance on its colonial subjects was a constant source of ridicule by the Germans.[27]

Many Allied leaders also had an aversion to pitting black soldiers against whites, fearing that this could undermine colonial racial hierarchies. The British refused to use African soldiers in Europe, though they employed many Africans in labor battalions. Likewise, the United States, a deeply segregated nation under the leadership of Woodrow Wilson, a racist, allowed very few African Americans to serve in combat, instead using most black soldiers as manual laborers.[28] However, massive casualties in the early months of the war convinced French officials of the need to utilize African soldiers heavily. Large numbers of the *Tirailleurs Sénégalais* were quickly transferred to the western front. Over the next four years, France raised an additional 500,000 colonial troops, from Algeria to Vietnam, including more than 160,000 West Africans. In Senegal, perhaps as many as a third of all males of military age served in the French Army during the war.[29]

Before the war, the *Tirailleurs Sénégalais* were mostly volunteers, but as France's need for African soldiers increased dramatically, wartime recruitment employed extremely coercive means. Conscripts were forcibly taken from villages by colonial officials, and bribes were paid to chiefs to supply their quota of recruits. Lamine Senghor was drafted during this period, which may account for his more pessimistic view of the war than Diallo's. In villages that resisted conscription, crops and livestock were seized and homes burned. To avoid the draft entire communities in French West Africa abandoned their homes and fled into neighboring colonies. The whole region was plunged into disarray,

---

27. For example, one of Germany's World War I propaganda pamphlets condemned the use of colonial soldiers in Europe: Auswärtiges Amt [German Foreign Office], *Employment, Contrary to International Law, of Colored Troops upon the European Arena of War by England and France* (Berlin, 1915).

28. For British and American attempts to limit the use of black troops in combat, see Glenford Howe, "West Indian Blacks and the Struggle for Participation in the First World War," *Journal of Caribbean History* 28 (1994): 33–49; and Jennifer D. Keene, *Doughboys, the Great War and the Remaking of America* (Baltimore: Johns Hopkins University Press, 2001), 40.

29. Das, *Race, Empire and First World War Writing*, 4; and Lunn, *Memoirs of the Maelstrom*, 224.

and rebellions against conscription and wartime taxation in Dahomey and Niger seriously challenged French rule. Finally, the military draft was discontinued in 1917 at the urging of the governor of French West Africa, Joost van Vollenhoven.[30]

West Africa's respite from conscription was short lived, as Georges Clemenceau reinstituted the draft in 1918, shortly after he became prime minister of France. Clemenceau was committed to a more efficient and aggressive management of the war, and Charles Mangin, the author of *La Force noire*, persuaded the prime minister that more African soldiers could help tip the balance in favor of France. During this round of conscription, however, the French authorities tread more carefully. Rather than relying so heavily on coercion, they enlisted the aid of Blaise Diagne, deputy for Senegal's Four Communes, who went on a recruitment drive throughout West Africa in 1918.[31]

Diagne was given powers equivalent to the governor-general as the commissioner of the Republic for West Africa, and he toured the colonies with an entourage of four hundred black soldiers who had served in France. The men were dressed in new uniforms with their military medals on display, and they were given special privileges only accorded Europeans, like traveling first class on trains. Diagne also sought the blessing of Muslim religious leaders and local chiefs, selling the conflict in Europe as a "war to obtain rights." Diagne held out the promise of French citizenship to Africans who served in the war and obtained military honors, like the Médaille Militaire and the Croix de Guerre. Diagne's mission was judged a great success, as it raised an additional sixty thousand West African soldiers for France.[32]

African Soldiers in Europe

In 1914, the *Tirailleurs Sénégalais* had been rushed to the western front, where they were thrown into battle against the Germans along the Marne River, in a determined effort to halt the enemy's advance on

---

30. Echenberg, *Colonial Conscripts*, 42; Lunn, *Memoirs of the Maelstrom*, 41–49; Mann, *Native Sons*, 68; and Glinga, "*Le tirailleur sénégalais*," 150–51.

31. C. M. Andrew and A. S. Kanya-Forstner, "France, Africa, and the First World War," *Journal of African History* 19, no. 1 (1978): 15.

32. Balesi, *From Adversaries to Comrades-in-Arms*, 92–95; and Lunn, *Memoirs of the Maelstrom*, 73–77.

Paris. Bakary Diallo was seriously wounded in this campaign. African soldiers were even more ill-prepared than their European counterparts for this new and deadly style of warfare. The *Tirailleurs Sénégalais* were less well equipped than French soldiers and had not been trained in the use of new weapons like machine guns, mortars, and grenades. Having experienced tremendous casualties, some African troops were diverted to the Balkans to fight against the Austrians and Bulgarians. Others remained in France, where they continued to man the trenches and where many participated in the catastrophic 1916 Somme offensive. French commanders believed that African units needed to be bolstered with "steadier" white soldiers. African battalions were usually mixed among white units at a ratio of 1:3.[33]

The Senegalese infantry suffered a tremendous death rate. There is even a debate about whether African troops were used as "cannon fodder" to spare the lives of French soldiers during the war. Some Africans suspected as much at the time, and the feeling has grown over the years. One of Diallo's Senegalese comrades claimed that "people see us as no more than hunting dogs to unleash on their prey" (pp. 145–46). Some historians, like Myron Echenberg and Charles Balesi, cast doubt on this idea since overall death rates for French (15.8 percent) and African (15.2 percent) soldiers were comparable. Other scholars, like Richard Fogarty and Joe Lunn, counter that West Africans were employed as "shock troops," exploiting the belief that black soldiers were more savage and bloodthirsty than whites. As Lunn notes, the 15 percent casualty rate is an average for the entire war, disguising the fact that casualties for Senegalese infantry were almost twice as high as for French infantry during the last two years of the war, 1917–1918. Lunn sees this as clear evidence that Africans were being disproportionately sacrificed in the final offensive assaults against the German lines.[34]

African soldiers also suffered from the unfamiliar cold and damp of French winters, but in this case, the military authorities tried to spare them the worst effects of the inclement weather. To restore the combat efficiency of the *Tirailleurs Sénégalais*, the French military

---

33. Balesi, *From Adversaries to Comrades-in-Arms*, 98; and William T. Dean III, "The French Colonial Army and the Great War," *The Historian* 76, no. 3 (Fall 2014): 479–517.

34. Balesi, *From Adversaries to Comrades-in-Arms*, 101–2; Echenberg, *Colonial Conscripts*, 46; Fogarty, *Race and War in France*, 85–86; and Lunn, *Memoirs of the Maelstrom*, 143–45.

instituted a practice called *hivernage* (from the French word for winter, *hiver*) in which African troops were shifted to special winter camps in the south of France. From October to February, African soldiers underwent drill and further military training at their winter camps, but also sometimes were employed as workers in munitions factories.[35] Diallo discusses one such camp, at Menton on the French Riviera, where he convalesced at a hospital for African soldiers.

While the winter camps were a welcome release from combat, African soldiers, unlike their French counterparts, were never given home leave to visit their families. Africa was just too far away to make this practical. French soldiers were eligible for leave every four months, but most Africans remained away from home for three to five years. Although separated from their family and friends, during the months of *hivernage*, African soldiers had greater opportunities to improve their French language skills and to mingle with French civilians.[36]

Many members of the white colonial elite had opposed sending Africans to Europe, fearing that it would give them aspirations above their station and lead to the erosion of racial boundaries. In fact, the war brought many African men into close, continuous contact with Europeans in ways that were unlikely in a colonial context.[37] *Strength and Goodness* chronicles many such encounters. French people became acquainted with Africans like Bakary Diallo as unique individuals rather than as racial stereotypes. Africans also were startled about certain aspects of European society.

African soldiers were surprised at how much friendlier people in France were toward them than in the colonies. This did not fail to leave an impression. Unlike colonial Africa or the United States, France had no color line or traditions of racial segregation to maintain. (This would come later.) Many African American soldiers who served overseas during the war also expressed shock at how well white people treated them in France. For some French people, Africans were an exotic novelty. Others expressed gratitude toward African soldiers and even invited them into their homes. Diallo relates many such incidents

---

35. Balesi, *From Adversaries to Comrades-in-Arms*, 100–102.

36. Balesi, *From Adversaries to Comrades-in-Arms*, 114; and Fogarty, *Race and War in France*, 206.

37. For racial interactions in colonial West Africa, see Rachel Jean-Baptiste, *Multi-Racial Identities in Colonial Francophone Africa: Race, Childhood, Citizenship* (Cambridge: Cambridge University Press, forthcoming).

in *Strength and Goodness*. This kind of interracial socializing rarely occurred in the colonies.[38]

Africans were also stunned to discover that some French people were poor and illiterate. Exposure to European class hierarchies was an eye-opening experience, as the very existence of poor white people contradicted the basis of colonial society. In Africa, whites never labored and "whiteness" automatically conferred privileged status. French peasants and workers especially seemed happy to treat Africans as equals. Fraternization between Africans and Europeans helped break down the color barrier, psychologically as well as physically, and suggested possibilities for a new political order after the war.

The one example of wartime cross-race friendships that raised eyebrows was that between African soldiers and French women, as this included the possibility of sex. The authorities limited contacts between black men and white women, fearful that miscegenation and mixed-race children would undermine colonial racial hierarchies.[39] While African soldiers were welcome to visit military brothels, officials hoped to minimize and police their contacts with "respectable" women. To this end, the government encouraged certain bourgeois women to act as *marraines de guerre* (wartime godmothers) by assisting colonial troops in adjusting to an unfamiliar society. These women were supposed to look after the welfare of African soldiers by writing letters for them, sending them gifts of food and clothing, visiting them in the hospital, and even inviting them into their homes.[40]

Some African soldiers later recalled that they were romantically involved with their *marraines* and that to them the term meant "girlfriend" as much as "godmother." The French women with whom Bakary Diallo associated tended to be adolescents, like Albertine Velty, whom he represented as sisters, or older women, like Marie Jullian, whom he thought of as mother figures. Whether Diallo was ever

38. Lunn, *Memoirs of the Maelstrom*, 176–79; and Balesi, *From Adversaries to Comrades-in-Arms*, 115–19.

39. For French attitudes about race mixing, see Emmanuelle Saada, *Empire's Children: Race, Filiation, and Citizenship in the French Colonies*, trans. Arthur Goldhammer (Chicago: University of Chicago Press, 2012).

40. Fogarty, *Race and War in France*, 206–7; and Balesi, *From Adversaries to Comrades-in-Arms*, 117–18. See also Tyler Stovall, "Love, Labor and Race: Colonial Men and White Women in France during the Great War," in *French Civilization and Its Discontents: Nationalism, Colonialism, Race*, ed. Tyler Stovall and Georges van den Abbeele (Lanham, MD: Lexington, 2003), 297–321.

sexually involved with a woman during his fourteen years in France, or whether he ever visited a brothel, we do not know. This would have been at odds with his strict Islamic values and, in any case, was not something he could have written about at the time. Other Senegalese soldiers in France mailed postcards to Africa of scantily clad or nude European women. The French authorities seized hundreds of such cards, fearing that this correspondence might undermine the "prestige" of white women in the colonies.[41]

Popular Images of African Soldiers

The *Tirailleurs Sénégalais* became stock figures in French popular culture during the war, though they were depicted in a wide variety of ways. Some posters, cartoons, and postcards portrayed African soldiers in patriotic and sentimental ways, often showing them as brave and loyal children of France, willing to die for the mother country. One widely disseminated poster, by French artist Lucien-Hector Jonas, showed African soldiers bravely charging into battle with their French comrades, heedless of oncoming German gunfire. A series of postcards entitled "Glory to Greater France," featured a young black soldier holding German helmets that he had captured in battle. (One of these postcards appears on the cover of this book.) As Richard Fogarty argues: "These images sought to reassure the French public that France had overseas support, to communicate the usefulness of the empire, and to remind viewers of the debt of gratitude they owed to the inhabitants of the colonies."[42]

Other images of African soldiers were somewhat risqué, exploiting the possibilities of romantic or sexual entanglements between the *Tirailleurs Sénégalais* and French women. Magazine illustrations and cartoons showed African soldiers flirting with French women, who seemed happy to receive their attentions. In one anthropomorphic cartoon, a black rabbit, dressed like a West African soldier, embraces

---

41. Lunn, *Memoirs of the Maelstrom*, 173; and Fogarty, *Race and War in France*, 219–22.

42. Richard S. Fogarty, "Race and Empire in French Posters of the Great War," in *Picture This: World War I Posters and Visual Culture*, ed. Pearl James (Lincoln: University of Nebraska Press, 2009), 174, 195–200.

"African Army and Colonial Forces Day." This 1917 French poster was designed by artist Lucien-Hector Jonas. African Army Day honored those colonial soldiers fighting in France.

a white rabbit. He tells her that "after the war, we'll go to Senegal and have many little *cafés au lait*" (coffees with milk, slang for mixed-race people). Many of these depictions had humorous overtones and expressed racist unease about miscegenation.[43]

Popular images of African soldiers also embodied racist clichés, frequently portraying them as headhunters and cannibals. Cartoons showed *Tirailleurs Sénégalais* collecting the ears or heads of German soldiers as souvenirs or roasting the Kaiser over an open fire. One postcard depicted an African soldier gleefully bayonetting a German

---

43. Many such images can be seen in Stephan Likosky, *With a Weapon and a Grin: Postcard Images of France's Black African Colonial Troops in WWI* (Atglen, PA: Schiffer Publishing, 2017), 59–66.

while asking him, "Do you want me to eat your flesh roasted or raw?"[44] French propaganda regarding the savagery of Africans was widely believed, both in France and abroad. Many French took comfort in the supposed barbarism of African soldiers, believing that they would massacre the Germans.[45] Diallo recalled that when he and his unit arrived in France in 1914, cheering crowds urged them to "Cut off the Germans' heads." (p. 108).

Racist representations of bestial Africans also served German interests. Germany criticized France for employing African soldiers against white people. After the war, when some Africans formed a part of the French Army of occupation in the German Rhineland, German politicians and journalists denounced this as *die schwarze Schande*, "the black shame." German propagandists falsely claimed that France deliberately chose African troops to humiliate Germans and that these soldiers were guilty of sexually assaulting German women. Some British imperialists and American segregationists sympathized with the German outcry over African troops, and even some progressives, like the socialist writers H. G. Wells and George Bernard Shaw, condemned France for using "savages" to police a "civilized" people. Stung by the international criticism, France withdrew African soldiers from the Rhineland in June 1920. The episode increased Germans' sense of victimhood in the postwar world and was later used by the Nazis as part of their racist propaganda.[46]

The most widely circulated image of an African soldier in France was "the y'a bon friend" (*l'ami y'a bon*), a smiling Senegalese rifleman used to advertise Banania, a popular chocolate drink that had been introduced in 1912. During the war, the product was marketed as a nutritious drink for soldiers, and in 1915 advertisements began featuring a happy African soldier drinking his morning cup of Banania. Gazing out at the viewer, he proclaims "y'a bon," broken French for "it

44. Likosky, *With a Weapon and a Grin*, 74–83.

45. Echenberg, *Colonial Conscripts*, 35.

46. Fogarty, *Race and War in France*, 275–76. For a detailed study of the Rhineland controversy, see Peter Collar, *The Propaganda War in the Rhineland: Weimar Germany, Race and Occupation after World War I* (London: I. B. Tauris, 2013); and Julia Roos, "Racist Hysteria to Pragmatic Rapprochement? The German Debate about Rhenish 'Occupation Children,' 1920–30," *Contemporary European History* 22, no. 2 (2013): 155–80.

good."[47] This trademark embodied the idea of the *Tirailleurs Sénégalais* as friendly buffoons and later was much condemned by black people. In a 1948 poem, Léopold Senghor, future president of independent Senegal, vowed: "I will tear off the banania grins from all the walls of France." In his 1952 book, *Black Skin, White Masks*, the Martiniquan writer Frantz Fanon speculated that when white people looked at him, they thought about "cannibalism, backwardness . . . and above all . . . the grinning Y'a bon Banania."[48] Nonetheless, the original advertising remains a cultural icon in France, with reproductions widely sold as posters, mugs, and refrigerator magnets.

"Banania—It Good"; a 1915 advertisement for the breakfast drink Banania. This was the most widely seen image of an African soldier in wartime France.

Having situated the military service of Bakary Diallo and other African soldiers within a wider context of French colonialism and the First World War, this introduction will next discuss Diallo's memoir in more detail, placing the book within the political and cultural currents of the postwar world of the 1920s.

---

47. Anne Donadey, "'Y'a bon Banania': Ethics and Cultural Criticism in the Colonial Context," *French Cultural Studies* 11, no. 31 (February 2000): 9–29.

48. Léopold Senghor, "Liminary Poem" in *Collected Poetry*, trans. Melvin Dixon (Charlottesville: University of Virginia Press, 1998), 39; and Frantz Fanon, *Black Skin, White Masks* (1952), trans. Richard Philcox (New York: Grove Press, 2008), 92.

Publication and Reception of
Force-Bonté/Strength and Goodness

Writing and publishing *Strength and Goodness* was a piece of good luck for Diallo. He spent more than a dozen years in France, convalescing from his wartime injuries and working a series of odd jobs. During this time he improved his spoken French and became literate in the language. In this endeavor, he was assisted by a number of French people, most notably Lucie Cousturier, a well-known French painter and daughter of a wealthy industrialist. Cousturier had a house and studio in southern France near Fréjus, where there were several winter camps for African soldiers. She befriended many of these men, organizing French language classes for them in her home. She wrote about this experience in her 1920 memoir, *Des inconnus chez moi* (*Strangers in My Home*), and later traveled in French Africa, about which she also wrote.[49] Cousturier took a special interest in Bakary Diallo. She may have encouraged him to write about his African childhood and wartime experiences, and, shortly before her death in 1925, she sent Diallo's manuscript of *Strength and Goodness* to her friend, the writer Jean-Richard Bloch. Bloch was a member of the French Communist Party and a veteran of the war, who, like Diallo, had been seriously wounded in combat. Bloch also had traveled widely in Africa and, like Cousturier, was committed to representing Africans as well-rounded individuals rather than as the cartoonish savages or happy buffoons so common in French depictions. Bloch worked at the progressive Rieder Press, which published *Strength and Goodness* in 1926.[50]

Strength and Goodness was widely and positively reviewed in the French press. The journal *France et Monde* praised it as a "new type of French literature" that revealed to the French people "the existence of a vast world beyond our borders." The reviewer saw this phenomenon as the natural development of colonialism, which had "revealed new horizons for many of the world's peoples." France's colonial subjects

49. On Lucie Cousturier, see Roger Little, ed., *Lucie Cousturier, les tirailleurs sénégalais et la question coloniale* (Paris: L'Harmattan, 2008).

50. On Jean-Richard Bloch, see Nancy Grey, "Jean-Richard Bloch," in *Jewish Writers of the Twentieth Century*, ed. Sorrel Kerbel (New York: Routledge, 2008), 91–93.

were now is a position to "do the same for us."[51] In an essay about
Africa, "The Black, a Blank Page," in *Les Nouvelles litteraires*, Pierre
Mille cited Diallo's "stunning, touching" book as evidence that blacks
"are men, just like us."[52] The Catholic journal *Revue des lectures*
expressed surprise that Diallo was able to maintain his faith in
"European civilization" despite "the thousands of minor insults" he
experienced in France. The review concluded that Diallo was "a good
black man" who had written a "good and decent" book but lamented
that no French person had ever tried to introduce him "to our religion,
the true religion of Jesus Christ."[53] Not surprisingly, reviewers were
less interested in evaluating *Strength and Goodness* as a distinct literary
work than in using the book to make some larger argument about
colonialism or race.

Many reviews of *Strength and Goodness* saw Bakary Diallo as the
modern-day embodiment of Jean-Jacques Rousseau's "noble savage,"
an uncivilized person who symbolized the innate goodness of those
not exposed to the corrupting influences of modern society. The
reviewer in the newspaper *Paris-soir* emphasized that Diallo was not
an "educated Negro" but "an authentic black man" from a "hut in
Senegal."[54] The journal *La Nouvelle revue socialiste* contrasted Diallo's
origin as "a simple Fula shepherd" with his "imagination" that was
"as rich as that of the most sophisticated white man." Diallo's book
revealed "the simple and affecting essence of his race," and "the delicate
sweetness of his heart."[55] A review essay, titled "The Beauty of a Black
Soul," from the newspaper *Comoedia* extolled Diallo as "a simple man,
who remained pure and natural." Invoking Rousseau, the reviewer
argued that although Diallo came from an "African tribe still wedded
to the pastoral way of life," he demonstrated "a better sense of right
and wrong . . . than we do, in our secular state."[56]

One reviewer not charmed by Bakary Diallo was Henri Barbusse,
whose own best-selling war memoir of 1916, *Le Feu* (*Under Fire*),

---

51. "Reviews," *France et Monde*, October 1926, 192, 256. This and the following
reviews of *Force-Bonté* from the 1920s were located and translated by Nancy Erber.

52. Pierre Mille, "The Black, a Blank Page," *Les Nouvelles litteraires*, September 29,
1926, 2.

53. "Novels," *Revue des lectures*, December 1, 1926, 867.

54. "Short Notes about Literature," *Paris-soir*, May 19, 1926, 2.

55. "Reviews," *La Nouvelle revue socialiste*, November 15, 1926, 499.

56. "The Beauty of a Black Soul," *Comoedia*, June 1926.

had famously deromanticized the war by depicting it as a savage and ruthless conflict. Now a pacifist and communist, Barbusse penned a scathing review of *Strength and Goodness* for the journal *L'humanité* in 1926. Entitled "Black Man with Rose-Colored Glasses Who Does Not Criticize War," the review sarcastically depicts Diallo as a naïve and "angelic" being who "finds goodness everywhere." At first "disarmed" by the author's optimism, Barbusse ultimately finds it "annoying." He ends his essay by directly addressing Diallo, urging him to reconsider his "depressing and unconvincing" praise of France and the war. Far from "a paradise of all human virtues," France was a greedy and corrupt society that had "exploited people abominably and inexcusably through colonialism," wasting the lives of black men in the World War. Until he woke up to this harsh reality, Diallo was "serving the cause of barbarism." At the time, Barbusse's harsh assessment stood alone, but, over the years, it came to predominate.[57]

In later decades black writers weighed in on Diallo's book. Among the first to discuss *Strength and Goodness* was the Caribbean novelist René Maran. Writing in the 1930s, Maran chided Diallo for his "sheepish conformism" and his "servility" to France. The African American scholar Edward Jones provided a more positive assessment in a 1948 essay on African literature. Jones expressed pride in a black writer who espouses "a religion of friendship among men of different races" but "never gives up his Africa and its heritage."[58] For the most part, however, *Strength and Goodness* was forgotten until the 1960s and 1970s, when there was a renewed academic interest in African culture, coinciding with African independence and the civil rights movement.

Postcolonial critics usually list Bakary Diallo among the pioneering Africans writing in French, but they are fairly contemptuous of his work. In her groundbreaking study *Black Writers in French* (1963), Lilyan Kesteloot glosses over *Strength and Goodness* as "merely a naïve panegyric to France," while O. R. Dathorne similarly dismisses Diallo

---

57. Henri Barbusse, "Black Man with Rose-Colored Glasses Who Does Not Criticize War," *L'humanité*, June 16, 1926, 4.

58. René Maran quoted in János Riesz and Aija Bjornson, "The *Tirailleur Sénégalais* Who Did Not Want to Be a 'Grand Enfant': Bakary Diallo's *Force Bonté* (1926) Reconsidered," *Research in African Literatures* 27, no. 4 (Winter 1996): 158; and Edward A. Jones, "Diallo and Senghor as Interpreters of the New French Africa," *French Review* 21, no. 6 (May 1948): 446.

as a writer who "merely sang of the splendors of France."[59] Literary scholars are frequently at a loss about how to treat *Strength and Goodness*, as it does not fit into the dominant postwar Negritude movement, in which black writers and artists celebrated a unique African-inflected culture, free from European influence. In the years since independence, many Africans, as well as Western critics of colonialism, found Diallo's expressions of French patriotism embarrassing, and they often ignored his work. In the words of one critic, *Strength and Goodness* remains "a skeleton in the African family closet."[60]

Some critics even questioned Diallo's authorship of *Strength and Goodness*, believing that its French was too polished and its politics too imperialist to have been written by an African. In *Black African Literature* (1966), Robert Pageard doubts that Diallo could have written the book as its "attitude of constant flattery" toward France was unlikely in an African.[61] Was *Strength and Goodness* perhaps ghostwritten or radically edited by Lucie Cousturier or Jean-Richard Bloch? In *African Literature in French* (1976), Dorothy Blair raises this possibility but seems to discount it, noting that Diallo was tutored in French by a sympathetic officer and later studied with Cousturier.[62] Such doubts are part of a long tradition in which white critics often questioned the authenticity of books written by black authors and credited those works to white patrons. For example, the authorship of earlier slave narratives by Mary Prince and Harriet Jacobs was doubted on the grounds that the women lacked the education and sophistication to compose such articulate works.[63]

In two critical essays from the 1970s, Fredric Michelman became the first scholar to treat *Strength and Goodness* seriously as a literary work. He praises the book's lyrical style and demonstrates how Diallo

---

59. Lilyan Kesteloot, *Black Writers in French: A Literary History of Negritude* (1963), trans. Ellen Conroy Kennedy (Philadelphia: Temple University Press, 1974), 10; and O. R. Dathorne, *The Black Mind: A History of African Literature* (Minneapolis: University of Minnesota Press, 1974), 266.

60. Fredric Michelman, "The Beginnings of French-African Fiction," *Research in African Literatures* 2, no. 1 (Spring 1971): 16.

61. Robert Pageard, *Littérature négro-africaine* (Paris: Livre Africain, 1966), 16.

62. Dorothy S. Blair, *African Literature in French* (Cambridge: Cambridge University Press, 1976), 16–17.

63. John Sekora discusses issues of authenticity in slave narratives in "Black Message/ White Envelope: Genre, Authenticity and Authority in the Antebellum Slave Narrative," *Callaloo* 32 (Summer 1987): 482–515.

articulates a sophisticated philosophy grounded in African cultural traditions. Michelman also points out important differences between Diallo's attitudes toward colonialism and those expressed in the writings of Cousturier and Bloch, countering the idea that one of them might have ghostwritten Diallo's book. Michelman argues that *Strength and Goodness* has exerted great influence over later African autobiographical writing, especially in its theme of "the uprooted hero irresistibly drawn to the city and often beyond to the marvels and disappointments of Europe." Nonetheless, Michelman understands how Diallo's "praise of France has made the book anathema to later generations of Africans."[64]

During the 1990s, Werner Glinga and János Riesz were among the first scholars to offer more nuanced and sympathetic readings of *Strength and Goodness*. Glinga emphasizes how Diallo aims to move beyond colonial dependency and to encourage Africans and French to "come to an understanding beyond the barriers of race, class or colonial status." Riesz rejects the longstanding view of Diallo as "a naïve apologist of French colonialism." He instead emphasizes Diallo's quest for personal dignity and his desire for universal peace and harmony among the different peoples of the world. To the extent that French civilization can help achieve universal equality, then Diallo sees it as a good thing. However, whenever colonialism throws up barriers between people, they must be broken down.[65]

Whether one views *Strength and Goodness* as naïvely patriotic or as radically egalitarian, or as some combination of the two, the book remains an important historical document and a rare firsthand account of colonialism and the First World War by an African. Debating Bakary Diallo's politics and allegiances will take us only so far. To fully appreciate the significance of Diallo's story, his book needs to be situated within the broader context of African culture, postwar colonial history, and the politics of the 1920s.

---

64. Fredric Michelman, "The Beginnings of French-African Fiction," 12, 14; and "The West African Novel Since 1911," *Yale French Studies* 53 (1976): 29–44.

65. Glinga, "*Le tirailleur sénégalais*," 149–71; and Riesz and Bjornson, "The *Tirailleur Sénégalais*," 157–79.

Race Politics after the War

Strength and Goodness was the product of a political moment in the 1920s when some Africans believed that their wartime sacrifices on behalf of France would translate into greater autonomy and equality. Bakary Diallo's book is full of yearnings for universal brotherhood. Another Senegalese soldier, Moctar Diallo, also expressed his hopes that the war would lead to "the disappearance forever of the miserable and mean-spirited questions over skin color and racial origins so that we can achieve universal peace, bringing with it fraternity, equality, and liberty."[66] Africans who had worked and fought for French victory were unwilling to return to their subject status once the war was over. Some, like Bakary Diallo, ultimately benefited from their wartime service. Others grew disillusioned and more critical of French rule.

Colonial soldiers frequently expressed pride in their military prowess as well as a new sense of political entitlement. Upon joining the French Army in 1914, the Senegalese schoolteacher Moumar Diallo wrote to a friend that before the war, the French looked upon us as "zeros," but "now we're equal before the law because we're soldiers just like them. We're going to spill our blood on French soil and then they'll know that we're the bravest of all their African subjects."[67] No less than twenty-five battalions of *Tirailleurs Sénégalais* were cited for heroic actions during the war.[68] Blaise Diagne had promised African soldiers greater equality in return for their bravery, but France was not always generous in victory. For example, Bakary Diallo's military decorations earned him French citizenship, but the army refused to pay him the same as a white soldier.

Some French leaders cynically employed the language of civic equality to recruit colonial peoples for the war, while others were genuinely committed to the ideals of universal rights. In July 1919, René-Boisneuf, a black deputy from Guadeloupe in the French West Indies, called attention to the United States Army's racist treatment of black soldiers. In response, his fellow lawmakers in the Chamber of Deputies passed a resolution affirming France's dedication to equality

---

66. Descamps et al., *Tirailleurs Sénégalais*, 54.

67. Descamps et al., *Tirailleurs Sénégalais*, 66.

68. Shelby Cullom Davis, *Reservoirs of Men: A History of the Black Troops of French West Africa* (Westport, CT: Negro Universities Press, 1970), 156.

and denouncing prejudice and racism. France was at least willing to pay lip service to the egalitarian principles of the French Revolution, though it was unwilling to seriously challenge racial inequality in its own overseas colonies.[69]

The other Allied nations were even less willing to endorse racial equality as part of a war supposedly fought for democracy. Woodrow Wilson endorsed national "self-determination" as one of his Fourteen Points, but, as a segregationist and white supremacist, he was only able to envision political independence for European peoples like Poles or Czechs, not for Africans or Asians. Likewise, Japan's desire for a declaration of racial equality in the League of Nations' Covenant was scuttled by the United States, Great Britain, and the British dominions of South Africa and Australia. The Australian prime minister, William Hughes, even threatened to mount a crusade throughout the "Anglo-Saxon" world against the declaration.[70]

When the 1919 Paris Peace Conference at Versailles, presided over by Wilson and the other Allied leaders, excluded black representatives, African American writer and activist W. E. B. DuBois organized a Pan-African Congress in Paris as a countermeasure. The Pan-African meeting, chaired by Blaise Diagne, involved black people from the United States, the Caribbean, and Africa.[71] With such a diverse group, consensus proved difficult. For example, when DuBois proposed that "Africa be ruled by Africans," the French West African delegates objected. They countered that they did not want independence but to be treated as French, "in the fullest sense that the term Frenchman implies." Diagne and his Senegalese allies were aiming for total equality *within the colonial system.*[72] Later generations of African nationalists have vilified Diagne as a collaborationist, but his position was fairly typical at the time. As the Senegalese scholar Mohamadou Kane explained in 1985, during the 1920s many Africans could not imagine

---

69. Fogarty, *Race and War in France*, 5.

70. Rolf Pfeiffer, "Exercises in Loyalty and Trouble-Making," *Australian Journal of Politics and History* 38, no. 2 (1992): 178.

71. For a discussion of the Pan-African Congress, see Sarah Claire Dunstan, "Conflicts of Interest: The 1919 Pan-African Congress and the Wilsonian Moment," *Callaloo* 39, no. 1 (January 2016): 133–50; and Margaret Macmillan, *Paris 1919: Six Months That Changed the World* (New York: Random House, 2003), 104–5.

72. Adriane Lentz-Smith, *Freedom Struggles: African Americans and World War I* (Cambridge, MA: Harvard University Press, 2009), 164; and Glinga, "*Le tirailleur sénégalais,*" 163.

colonialism "to be mortal" and "believed it to be established for all eternity."[73]

Bakary Diallo, like Blaise Diagne, hoped to participate more fully in colonial society. Diallo wanted the same rights and privileges of French citizenship already enjoyed by the *originaires* of Senegal's Four Communes. His military service and decorations entitled him to this. As historian Gregory Mann recently argues, *Strength and Goodness* was the first work by an African that invokes "a critical language of political entitlement." Addressed to a sympathetic European audience, the book was a plea for equality and fair treatment.[74] In the final chapter, Diallo invokes the many African soldiers "buried in French soil." He thought that "their graves represent a serious moral guarantee" of French goodwill (p. 162). Many African veterans adopted a similar strategic position, demanding that France fulfill its wartime promises to them and live up to the republican ideals of equality and brotherhood.

In the postwar years, African veterans developed a new political language of sacrifice and entitlement, claiming that the French state owed them for their military service. Ex-soldiers from the war were often feared as a disruptive element in colonial West Africa. As Werner Glinga argues, "The *tirailleur* was to become a new social figure in African society, an element of unrest, difficult to control, and very demanding." In 1919, as returning veterans journeyed from coastal African towns to their inland villages, they demanded that the locals feed and house them for free. They sometimes seized cattle for themselves and insulted village elders, calling them "ignorant" and "savage."[75]

The French state did grant privileges to African veterans, and in this they stood out among their allies. Veterans and their families were exempt from certain taxes and labor obligations, and they had access to preferential employment opportunities. Ex-soldiers secured desirable positions in the colonial administration as police, interpreters, clerks, and office workers. Among the few Africans who had experienced European society firsthand, veterans acted as go-betweens in colonial culture. During the 1920s, veterans came to fill leadership roles at the

---

73. Mohamadou Kane, introduction to *Force-Bonté* (Paris: Nouvelles Éditions Africaines, 1985), xi.

74. Mann, *Native Sons*, 202, 290n72.

75. Glinga, "*Le tirailleur sénégalais*," 151; and Mann, *Native Sons*, 64–65, 77.

village level that had previously been held by traditional chiefs. Bakary Diallo himself benefited from such career opportunities in the colonial service, ultimately achieving the position of *chef de canton*, or district chief, an administrative rank rarely given to Africans.[76]

Not all African veterans felt adequately repaid for their wartime service to France. Many, unlike Diallo, did not get full citizenship rights. Their pensions were much smaller than those received by white veterans and often were not paid regularly. French promises that black participation in the war would lead to reform of colonial government were not kept, leading to disillusionment and feelings of betrayal. In postwar Senegal, veterans were prominent in organizing the colony's first trade unions and political parties. Some West African veterans even became radical nationalists and demanded independence.[77]

Lamine Senghor emerged during the 1920s as the best-known African anti-colonial activist. Like Bakary Diallo, he had served in France with the *Tirailleurs Sénégalais* and was seriously wounded in combat. Unlike Diallo, his disenchantment with France grew in the years following the war. Senghor joined the French Communist Party and founded the Universal League for the Defense of the Negro Race to demand full citizenship rights for Africans living under French rule. During the 1920s, Senghor served alongside the Vietnamese nationalist Ho Chi Minh in the Intercolonial Union, a communist organization which sought to dismantle the French Empire.[78]

For Senghor World War I represented the worst example of imperial exploitation. In 1924, he published an article in the left-wing journal *Le Paria* denouncing the war and Blaise Diagne's role in promoting it. In the article, Senghor fantasized about parading before Diagne a "procession of blind and mutilated soldiers: those whose faces are horribly disfigured, those who suffer from atrocious internal pain, and

---

76. Glinga, "*Le tirailleur sénégalais*," 149, 163; and Mann, *Native Sons*, 71, 86–87.

77. Lunn, *Memoirs of the Maelstrom*, 84, 194–96; and Glinga, "*Le tirailleur sénégalais*," 163. For nationalist activities by veterans in another part of Africa, see James K. Matthews, "World War I and the Rise of African Nationalism: Nigerian Veterans as Catalysts of Change," *Journal of Modern African Studies* 20, no. 3 (1982): 493–502.

78. On Lamine Senghor, see David Murphy, "Defending the 'Negro Race': Lamine Senghor and Black Internationalism in Interwar France," *French Cultural Studies* 24, no. 2 (2013): 161–73. For a good general history of African and Asian nationalism in postwar France, see Michael Goebel, *Anti-Imperial Metropolis: Interwar Paris and the Seeds of Third World Nationalism* (Cambridge: Cambridge University Press, 2015).

the orphans and widows." These African victims of the war would then spit in Diagne's face.[79]

In 1927, the year he died, Senghor published *The Rape of a Country*, an anti-imperial pamphlet that denounced France's exploitation of Africans in a world war fought to benefit Western capitalism. That same year Senghor cemented his reputation as the foremost African anti-colonialist in a speech he gave at the first meeting of the League Against Imperialism in Brussels. Senghor assured the audience that "black youth now see clearly. We know that when we are needed, to make us fight or to make us work, we are French; but when it comes to giving us rights, we are no longer French, we are just Negroes."[80]

The biographies of Bakary Diallo and Lamine Senghor represent radically divergent paths taken by two young men from Senegal who served in the French Colonial Army during World War I. Diallo's accommodation with colonialism was more typical than Senghor's advocacy of revolution, but over time, especially after World War II, growing numbers of West African veterans came to support independence from French rule. And yet, even after Senegal's independence in 1960, West African veterans continued to express pride in their contributions to the war and to Allied victory. For years afterward they took part in Armistice Day parades in Dakar. Elderly African veterans interviewed in the 1970s and 1980s still spoke fondly of their military service.[81]

Later generations of Africans, especially those born after independence, feel differently about the Great War. Many are now embarrassed by their ancestors' service in the French Army, which they prefer to downplay or which they recast wholly in terms of exploitation. Many World War I monuments in French Africa have been dismantled, sent back to France, or moved from prominent positions to the outskirts of African towns.[82] Likewise, Africans now

---

79. Glinga, "*Le tirailleur sénégalais*," 159.

80. Senghor, *La Violation d'un pays et autres écrits anticolonialistes*, 63.

81. For example, in 1974 Charles John Balesi interviewed more than forty West African veterans of the Great War, all of whom expressed pride in their military service. *From Adversaries to Comrades-in-Arms*, 117.

82. For a discussion of the generational divide over the war, see Joe Lunn, "France's Legacy to Demba Mboup? A Senegalese Griot and His Descendants Remember His Military Service during the First World War," in Das, *Race, Empire and First World War Writing*, 117–19. On African war memorials, see Likosky, *With a Weapon and a Grin*, 109.

deride *Strength and Goodness* for its patriotic stance, or else try to forget it altogether. In this regard, they are not that different from many Europeans who, in the decades following the First World War, have become increasingly disenchanted with that conflict.[83]

La Vogue Nègre and the War Books Craze

The publication of *Strength and Goodness* in 1926 was part of two postwar cultural phenomena that help to explain its appeal. The first, *La Vogue Nègre* (the Negro fashion), refers to a fascination with African culture, broadly defined, in 1920s Paris. The second, the "war books" craze, refers to an explosion of memoirs and novels about the First World War throughout the Western world during the late 1920s. Most of these books were written by veterans, and they tended to depict the war in a harsher light than had the patriotic propaganda of the previous decade.

The postwar craze for African art and culture helped create an audience for works like *Strength and Goodness*. During the war, African American musicians, like James Reese Europe and Noble Sissle, popularized jazz in France. Some of these musicians stayed on after the war, enjoying France's more racially inclusive atmosphere and performing "le hot jazz" at Parisian nightclubs. Contemporary avant-garde artists, like Pablo Picasso and Henri Matisse, produced so-called primitivist paintings inspired by West African masks, sculptures, and fabric that had entered France through colonial trade. This newfound passion for "black" culture inspired a Negrophile movement that played on white European fantasies of Africans as exotic and primitive—more in touch with their basic instincts. Through immersion in the art and music of black people, some Europeans

83. Among the many works about European disillusionment with World War I, see Paul Fussell, *The Great War and Modern Memory* (New York: Oxford University Press, 1975); George L. Mosse, *Fallen Soldiers: Reshaping the Memory of the World Wars* (Oxford: Oxford University Press, 1990); and Jay Winter, *Sites of Memory, Sites of Mourning: The Great War in European Cultural History* (Cambridge: Cambridge University Press, 1995).

hoped to rekindle their own more "natural" selves, repressed by an overly disciplined industrial society.[84]

In 1926, the year *Strength and Goodness* was published, *La Revue Nègre*, a jazz musical revue featuring black performers from the United States, took Paris by storm. The charismatic star of the show was Josephine Baker, who performed an eroticized dance in a banana skirt to the beat of a tom-tom.[85] Bakary Diallo, a serious thinker and a strict Muslim, would no doubt have been appalled by this travesty of African culture, but in the minds of many French people, he and Baker were part of the same fad. Indeed, a front page article by Alfred Guignard in the popular newspaper *Le Gaulois* paired Baker and Diallo. Under the headline "Black Stars," Guignard proclaimed: "Our brothers of the black race are popular." While Josephine Baker represented "the female side" with her "spectacular debut on stage," Bakary Diallo represented "those magnificent black soldiers" whose "unsung heroics" aided France's victory in the Great War. Having "transformed his bayonet into a pen," Diallo's "beautiful book" was yet another effusion of the African spirit.[86]

The publication of *Strength and Goodness* also coincided with a postwar explosion of books about World War I. In the decade following the war, once the initial shock and period of mourning had passed, the public was hungry for vivid, firsthand accounts of the conflict to counter the patriotic propaganda and heavily censored reportage that had been available during the war. While most literary scholars treat *Strength and Goodness* as a pioneering work of African literature, it should also be considered as part of the war book craze of the 1920s.[87]

Bakary Diallo's memoir was one of hundreds of war books, mostly penned by veterans, that appeared between the mid-1920s and the

---

84. On the French postwar fascination with African culture, see Petrine Archer-Straw, *Negrophilia: Avant-Garde Paris and Black Culture in the 1920s* (London: Thames and Hudson, 2000).

85. For Josephine Baker's life, see Phyllis Rose, *Jazz Cleopatra: Josephine Baker in Her Time* (New York: Doubleday, 1989); and Jennifer Anne Boittin, *Colonial Metropolis: The Urban Grounds of Anti-Imperialism and Feminism in Interwar Paris* (Lincoln: University of Nebraska Press, 2010), 1–36.

86. Alfred Guinard, "Black Stars," *Le Gaulois*, October 4, 1926, 1.

87. On the phenomenon of the war books, see Cyril Falls, *War Books: A Critical Guide* (London: P. Davies, 1930); and Philip E. Hager and Desmond Taylor, eds., *The Novels of World War I: An Annotated Bibliography* (New York: Garland, 1981).

early 1930s. Among the most famous and best remembered of these works, are Jaroslav Hašek's *The Good Soldier Švejk* (1923), Ford Maddox Ford's *No More Parades* (1925), Arnold Zweig's *The Case of Sergeant Grischa* (1928), Richard Aldington's *Death of a Hero* (1929), Robert Graves's *Good-bye to All That* (1929), Ernest Hemingway's *A Farewell to Arms* (1929), Erich Maria Remarque's *All Quiet on the Western Front* (1929), Louis-Ferdinand Céline's *Journey to the End of the Night* (1932), and Vera Brittain's *Testament of Youth* (1933). Many of these books straddled literary genres, either as novels heavily based on personal experiences, like *All Quiet . . .* , or as memoirs that employed novelistic devices, like *Good-bye to All That* and *Strength and Goodness*. For example, like Robert Graves, Diallo frequently includes in his memoir detailed wartime conversations that necessarily entailed imaginative reconstructions.

Most of the war books also radically challenged the public's rather sanitized view of the war by presenting it as a brutal slaughter, exposing readers to the gruesome details of trench warfare and the deadly consequences of military blunders by incompetent generals. This literature seriously undermined a venerable Western tradition of depicting war as a chivalrous and heroic adventure. The war books contributed to a growing sense of disillusionment with the Great War, since the conflict had not ushered in a new era of peace and prosperity, as wartime propaganda had promised. Those war books that continued to uphold more conventional and patriotic views, like Ernest Raymond's *Tell England* (1922), Robert McClure's *Some Found Adventure* (1926), and Bakary Diallo's *Strength and Goodness* (1926), have fallen out of favor as the pessimistic view of World War I has only grown over time.[88]

Although the war books were part of an international publishing phenomenon, they overwhelmingly represented the viewpoints of Europeans and Americans. No war books were penned by any of the Japanese, Indian, Arab, or Turkish veterans of the war, and only one by an African, Bakary Diallo, which has perpetuated the erroneous view that World War I was a European war. Westerners sometimes included *Tirailleurs Sénégalais* as characters in their war books, though usually as

---

88. For connections between the war books and postwar disillusionment, see Fussell, *The Great War and Modern Memory*; and Bernard Bergonzi, *Heroes' Twilight: A Study of the Literature of the Great War* (London: Constable, 1965).

racist caricatures. In *Good-bye to All That*, for instance, Robert Graves depicts African soldiers as savages who collected German heads as souvenirs.[89] Even when writers attempted a sympathetic depiction of a Senegalese rifleman, as brothers Jérôme and Jean Tharaud did in their novel, *The Long Walk of Samba Diouf* (1922), their protagonist was based on anthropological research rather than firsthand experience.[90] *Strength and Goodness* therefore remains important as a realistic autobiographical account by an African soldier in the Great War and as a testament to the significant, but mostly forgotten, African contributions to that war.

Bakary Diallo's Worldview

As the publication of Bakary Diallo's memoir is linked to many of the political and cultural developments of his era, so too are the ideas and philosophy expressed in the book. Few people who have written about *Strength and Goodness* take Diallo seriously as a writer or a thinker. Those who praised Diallo in the 1920s viewed him as a noble savage, while his later critics dismissed him as a naïve admirer of France. Both of these views are rather patronizing, imaging Diallo as simple and childlike. In fact, *Strength and Goodness* expounds a well-articulated philosophy of equality and the connections among all humanity. Nor should we see this worldview, as Jean-Richard Bloch did in 1926, as the "natural goodness" that sprang from "the native fragrance of the black soul."[91] Far from a timeless and essentialist creed grounded in race, Diallo's philosophy emerged from specific historical circumstances and cultural influences.

There is no doubt that Bakary Diallo was a French patriot. He never questions the war in Morocco, insisting that "the Moroccans simply must recognize the great benefit being offered to them" (p. 95). When World War I begins, Diallo assumes that France is in the right and stands for enlightenment and justice. After all, "France has a noble heart and a spirit of absolute fairness" (p. 96). While remarks like these have caused some critics to dismiss *Strength and Goodness*

---

89. Robert Graves, *Good-bye to All That* (London: Jonathan Cape, 1929), 237–38.

90. Jérôme and Jean Tharaud, *The Long Walk of Samba Diouf* (1922), trans. Willis Steell (New York: Doubleday, 1924).

91. Bloch, introduction to *Force-Bonté* (Paris: Rieder, 1926).

as a sycophantic hymn to France, the book also includes examples of colonial injustice and racism. One of Diallo's fellow soldiers argues that "the French are too arrogant. They think they're better than everyone else" (p. 96). Elsewhere, Diallo gives instances of "the double-dealing" and "the pettiness of the military authorities'" (p. 152) treatment of him, as when a French officer sentences him to eight days in jail for complaining about the hospital food that he was unable to eat because of his shattered jaw (p. 133).

Rather than seeing Bakary Diallo as someone who embraces European civilization uncritically, he should be seen as trying to negotiate between two cultures.[92] He credits France with ending internecine tribal warfare in Senegal but also praises heroes of African history, like Al Hadj Umar, a nineteenth-century Fula king who resisted French invaders (p. 70). More provocatively, when Diallo visited Dagana in 1911, he made a pilgrimage to the tomb of Ali Diop, a Muslim holy man who had led an uprising against French rule in 1908. After Diallo is wounded, he rejects his *gris-gris* (charm) in favor of modern medicine but elsewhere expresses his admiration for African music and storytelling. Most significantly, Diallo does not abandon Islam for Christianity but remains a devout Muslim all his life. Although Diallo believed that Africa could gain much from its association with France, he was not a total assimilationist. As the Senegalese sergeant Amidou Frama argues in *Strength and Goodness*, Africans could keep the good things they learned from France and discard the rest, "just as you pick through a heap of peas to keep the ones that are good to eat and discard the pebbles" (p. 146).

While Bakary Diallo's Francophilia glossed over the worst aspects of imperialism, his impassioned commitment to racial equality was uncompromising and, in the political context of the 1920s, quite radical. In the years following the war, there was a worldwide upsurge of racial violence, as European imperialists and American white supremacists reasserted their dominance and repudiated wartime promises of greater democracy.[93] Diallo, however, remains steadfastly committed to a color-blind world and argues throughout *Strength*

---

92. Werner Glinga argues that Diallo is trying to reconcile his admiration for France with his pride in Senegalese culture. Glinga, "*Le tirailleur sénégalais*," 460–62.

93. For the upsurge in racial violence after World War I, see Jacqueline Jenkinson, *Black 1919: Riots, Racism and Resistance in Imperial Britain* (Liverpool: Liverpool University Press, 2009); and Lentz-Smith, *Freedom Struggles*, 194–96.

and Goodness that it was pointless "to pretend to be superior to one's neighbor since we are all made the same" (p. 93).

Early in the book, when Diallo leaves his village for the city of Saint-Louis, he expresses sadness at how the different races are separated by language and skin color—not only the Africans and Europeans, but within Senegal, the brown-skinned Fula and the black-skinned Wolof. As Diallo mixes with different peoples in the town, and later in the army, where Africans from different ethnic groups and social strata served together, he starts to question racial categories. Soon Diallo insists that "the Fula and the Wolof actually should be united, as should all human beings" since "human nature" was the same in all people regardless of skin color (p. 66).

A central theme of *Strength and Goodness* is the superficiality and insignificance of racial and cultural markers like skin color, language, or dress. Whether people wore "African robes or European suits," they are "just as worthwhile" (pp. 126–27). More important than a person's skin color is "the quality of the spirit that is the guiding light" (p. 145). Europeans and Africans needed to look beyond superficial racial markers and recognize a common humanity. "Our skin color makes people suspicious when they don't bother looking past the surface, the exterior. However, color shouldn't mislead and blind us to the true inner essence of things and people" (p. 150). Diallo concludes his book with a plea for unity and love between the races: "Let's all work together without any racial divisions. Color is on the outside, and we know that we are profoundly affected by goodness inside our bodies and cruelty only on the outside. Let's all love each other, despite the superficial prejudices meant to keep us apart" (p. 162).

In its most radical formulation, *Strength and Goodness* insists not only on the equality of all peoples but on the fundamental unity of the universe, and all its creatures. The book frequently extols the beauties of nature while also expressing sorrow at how war desecrates "Mother Earth" and how humans mistreat animals. When Diallo's fellow soldiers divert themselves by fishing, he laments that the fish "die suffocating in the hot sun, strangling on the hooks that awful men have invented" (p. 101). In another passage, Diallo pities a group of horses powering a water pump by trudging endlessly in circles. He argues that we treat animals "like slaves" since they are unable to communicate their feelings to us. When his friend Demba replies that even if animals could talk, people would still dominate them because we are more powerful, Diallo insists that we should not be blinded by self-interest. Demba agrees that "we're all put on this earth to help each other" and further ponders that perhaps one day the "poor downtrodden" animals "will become our masters, and our superior status today will come to an end" (p. 83). Demba's musings might represent traditional animist beliefs but could also serve as an analogy for imperialism.

The intellectual underpinnings of Bakary Diallo's egalitarian and universalist worldview remain uncertain, since his views appear fully formed in his memoir, with little discussion of his cultural background or influences. Nonetheless, we can infer influence, since many of Diallo's ideas had much in common with several aspects of contemporary African and European society. Fredric Michelman believes that Diallo's universalism sprang from "a fundamental animism" underlying traditional African culture, whereby divine spirits were thought to inhabit much of the natural world. Werner Glinga thinks that Diallo was inspired by the Fula concept of "*molsdiéré*," a natural "goodness" that resides in all people.[94] Diallo's philosophy also has much in common with the Fula ethical code, or *Pulaaku*, which emphasizes the interdependence of people and the natural world as well as tolerance and respect for others.[95]

During Bakary Diallo's youth, Senegal was heavily influenced by Sufism, a spiritual movement within Islam that emphasizes the divine unity of the world. Sufis de-emphasize religious law and divine judgment, instead stressing God's love and the importance of individuals cultivating a mystical union with God. The most influential Sufi spiritual leader in early twentieth-century Senegal, Amadou Bamba, had founded the Mouride Brotherhood in 1883. The Mourides accepted French rule, downplaying politics in favor of service to humanity and economic autonomy. Nonetheless, Bamba preached the absolute equality of all people before God—a strong counter to the racist claims of Europeans. It is probably not a coincidence that Diallo's ideology has much in common with Bamba's.[96]

---

94. Michelman, "The Beginnings of French-African Fiction," 12; and Glinga, "*Le tirailleur sénégalais*," 161.

95. For a discussion of *Pulaaku*, see P. Riesman, *Freedom in Fulani Social Life* (Chicago: University of Chicago Press, 1998), 125–41.

96. For the influence of Sufism and the Mouride Brotherhood, see Leonardo A. Villalón, *Islamic Society and State Power in Senegal* (Cambridge: Cambridge University Press, 1995).

Lastly, Diallo's universalist ideas are bound up with the interwar peace movement, with which he clearly sympathized. The unprecedented casualties of World War I, in which more than ten million soldiers and several million civilians died, led to a widespread revulsion against war during the 1920s. This sentiment was channeled into support for the League of Nations, dedicated to the peaceful resolution of conflict, and other organizations devoted to pacifism or international cooperation such as the World Peace Foundation and the Women's International League for Peace and Freedom.[97] Diallo associated with a number of French internationalists, like Jean-Richard Bloch, and in *Strength and Goodness*, he argues that "we should applaud the men and women who are working to establish the principle of world peace" (p. 89).

Although Bakary Diallo supported the French cause during the Great War, he still saw war as a "tragedy" that "buries us alive in an abyss of suffering" (pp. 132, 124). He believed that wars were caused by misunderstandings and the inability of different peoples to communicate with one another. Diallo fantasized about "a universal language" (p. 89) but also believed that war could be avoided "if human beings would only use respect and admiration in their dealings with one another" (p. 124). Racial and ethnic prejudice must be eliminated, so that nations could base their judgments "on facts alone" instead of bigotry.

One hundred years after World War I, Bakary Diallo's dream of a color-blind world has yet to become a reality. His advocacy of racial equality and respect for all people remains relevant today, when ethnic and racial violence is proliferating around the world. Diallo's vivid and dignified portraits of the African soldiers of the Great War also help rescue these men from historical neglect and racist clichés. By taking Africans seriously and by placing them at the center of world historical events, *Strength and Goodness* testifies to the connections between colonialism and World War I and supports justice for the peoples of Africa.

---

97. For the history of movements for world peace and international cooperation during the 1920s, see Peter Brock and Thomas P. Socknat, eds., *Challenge to Mars: Essays on Pacifism from 1918 to 1945* (Toronto: University of Toronto Press, 1999); Daniel Gorman, *The Emergence of International Society in the 1920s* (Cambridge: Cambridge University Press, 2012); and Terry M. Mays, "Peacekeeping under the League of Nations," *Global War Studies* 10 (2013): 38–55.

Note on Translations

The title of Bakary Diallo's memoir, *Force-Bonté*, is not a common French expression, and it is difficult to render into English. The French word *force* (strength) serves as an adjective modifying *bonté* (goodness), so that the most literal English title would be *Powerful Goodness*. We have chosen *Strength and Goodness* as less awkward sounding. The scholar Werner Glinga suggests that *Force-Bonté* was Diallo's attempt to convey in French the Fula word *molsdiéré*, meaning the very best behavior that each person is capable of.

We have translated the *Tirailleurs Sénégalais* in which Diallo served as "Senegalese Infantrymen." Despite the name *tirailleurs* (literally, riflemen), they were foot soldiers, and they were not exclusively from Senegal. Instead, this indigenous force was recruited from across French West Africa and French Equatorial Africa. As infantrymen, they were trained in hand-to-hand combat. Infantry units typically bore the brunt of modern warfare and suffered the greatest casualties, and the colonial forces in World War I were no exception.

Strength and Goodness, often acknowledged as the first full-length prose work published in French by an African author, is written in a straightforward style. Yet Bakary Diallo often mixed present and past tenses in his recollections, and in our translation we have tried to keep the verbs in their original forms, even though that may sometimes be awkward in English. We have, however, altered the original chapter divisions, breaking the last one, Chapter 10, into six shorter chapters that are similar in length to the first nine. The author's original subheadings provide the titles for these new chapters.

Diallo occasionally incorporated words or expressions from his native language, Fula, and those of his *tirailleur* comrades into his narrative, and we have included explanatory notes of them in the text. Diallo also presented snippets of conversation between French officers and himself; these were rendered in the simplified French variety called at the time *petit nègre*. The French War Department actually codified this variety in a manual published in 1916 for officers' use. This manual, which has been digitized by the French National Library, was an invaluable source for clarifying some of the idiosyncrasies of Diallo's prose, which was no doubt influenced by his first exposure to this variety of French used as a spoken, contact language in Africa. As we know, after the war Diallo continued to develop his linguistic skills, first in France and later in Senegal, where he served as a translator for the French colonial government.

—Nancy Erber and William Peniston

Glossary

African Words

djamas: mosques
djéré: marketplace
djimis: songs
gorko: status of adult man; one who has completed initiation into manhood
griot: person from the caste of poets, singers, and historians
gris-gris: amulets or good luck charms
guédj: the sea
labbo: person from the caste of woodworkers and carpenters
marabout: Muslim holy man
molsdiéré: goodness; the utmost good that each person is able to perform
saourou: shepherd's staff

French Words

coupe-coupe (cut-cut): short saber carried by the *Tirailleurs Sénégalais*
hivernage (wintering): French military practice of withdrawing African soldiers from the western front during the winter (November–April) and stationing them in the south of France
tirailleurs (riflemen): West African infantry in the service of the French colonial state

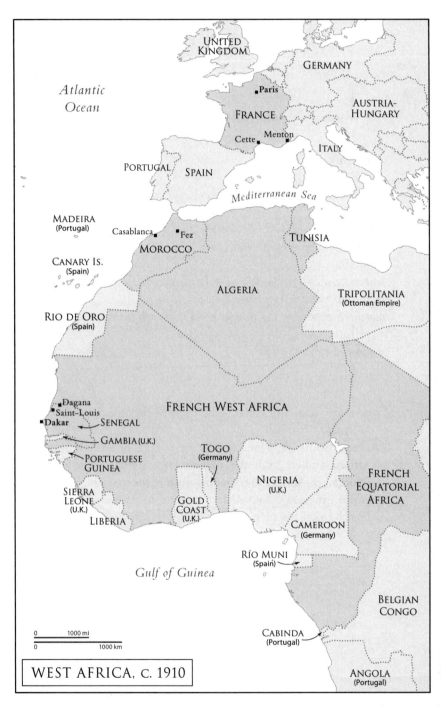

UNITED
KINGDOM

GERMANY

Atlantic
Ocean

■Paris

FRANCE

AUSTRIA-
HUNGARY

Cette■ ■Menton

ITALY

PORTUGAL SPAIN

Mediterranean Sea

MADEIRA
(Portugal)

Casablanca■ ■Fez

MOROCCO

TUNISIA

CANARY IS.
(Spain)

ALGERIA

TRIPOLITANIA
(Ottoman Empire)

RÍO DE ORO
(Spain)

■Dagana
■Saint-Louis
■Dakar   SENEGAL

FRENCH WEST AFRICA

GAMBIA (U.K.)

PORTUGUESE
GUINEA

TOGO
(Germany)

NIGERIA
(U.K.)

FRENCH
EQUATORIAL
AFRICA

SIERRA
LEONE
(U.K.)

GOLD
COAST
(U.K.)

LIBERIA

CAMEROON
(Germany)

RÍO MUNI
(Spain)

Gulf of Guinea

BELGIAN
CONGO

0   1000 mi

0   1000 km

CABINDA
(Portugal)

WEST AFRICA, C. 1910

ANGOLA
(Portugal)

44

Strength and Goodness

)(

Bakary Diallo

Writers in France, and in all countries, I salute you.
Your pens, with a simple stroke, bring light on us here on earth
in the evolution of human thought.

—Bakary Diallo

1.

My Childhood

I WAS BORN IN 1892 IN M'BALA, DAGANA CIRCUIT, SENEGAL.[1] I'm a Fula.[2] From my earliest childhood, my parents insisted that I was going to be a shepherd. Among my people, a cattle herder or a shepherd for sheep, or even goats, is an esteemed person. That's understandable because the Fula's only wealth is in their flocks and these animals represent all that you could hope for in terms of riches. Raising and grazing animals are the most important occupations for the Fula, even today. Thus, as soon as my parents saw that I was able to hold a *saourou* [shepherd's staff], they had me take over the job of herding their sheep. I undertook a task that was very difficult for me, if I may say so, because even though I felt glad and proud to obey my parents, I didn't at all enjoy being a shepherd.

Instead, my eyes were drawn to the sight of the constellations in the sky. I loved the stars more than anything else in the heavens. So it often happened in the evening that I'd return to my village without even a single animal from my flock because I had been distracted by the sight of those natural wonders. To the great satisfaction of wolves and hyenas, I would lose track of my flock and could only recover it after many a frantic search. Of course,

1. The French subdivided their African colonies into *cercles* (circuits). Dagana Circuit was in northern Senegal.

2. The Fula (also called Fulani or Fulbe) are the second largest ethnic group in Senegal, after the Wolof. Traditionally nomadic herdsmen, they live in northeastern Senegal, as well as in several other West African nations. The French referred to the Fula as Peulh (or Peul), which is the term Diallo used. We are using Fula, as it is the most common term employed in English today.

my father repaid me handsomely with the *saourou*, which is the
symbol of the shepherd's honor among us Fula. That meant I hadn't
been doing my duty as my fellow Fula had done. It is clear that I
was punished by losing my honor as much as by the blows raining
down on me from that dreadful stick.

My mother, who was very sensitive and who loved me dearly,
couldn't hide all the pain she was feeling. Her agony, quite visible
on her beloved face, broke my heart.

According to our customs, a boy officially becomes a man at the
age of sixteen. On that occasion we hold a big celebration that is
fun for people but not for sheep and cattle. The people dance and
the animals are slaughtered to mark the day when a Fula youth puts
on his first pair of trousers. Finally the long-awaited day comes . . .
I ask my father if I can wear trousers this year. He replies gravely
that I could, but that he would not organize a celebration in honor
of a son who doesn't deserve one. I discuss this with my mother,
who sends me to her brother, my uncle, a great fellow. He gives
me two head of superb cattle; by that I mean, really big ones.

I head to Gasba-Podor to buy enough silk to make a *boubou*[3] as
well as lots of other little things. I arrive in town. I sell my cattle
and in return receive some gold coins imprinted with the head
of Napoleon. I go to the store owned by the man we call Ax, the
biggest shopkeeper in Podor, and there I see a girl with golden
blond hair and blue eyes. It's the first time I had ever seen a white
woman. There, right before my eyes, are people paler than any I've
seen.[4] I'm amazed. I watch them and listen to them speak; since I
don't understand anything they say, I'm even more stunned.

---

3. A *boubou* is a loose garment that resembles a gown. It is traditional clothing for
both men and women.

4. Elsewhere Diallo refers to the peoples of Senegal having different skin colors, with
the Fula being lighter complected than the Wolof.

I realize I should ask about these people's race, and a black man who works in the shop tells me: "They're called French, my boy. And where do you come from?" "From M'Bala, Sovanabé-Botol," I reply.[5] He looks at me for a long time and then asks: "So is this the first time you've come here, my friend?" "Yes," I say. After a short, silent pause, he continues: "Some of them are good, intelligent."

Having made my purchases, I go back to M'Bala, ready to become an adult, according to my people's customs.

My father, who never changed his mind, refused to have anything to do with the celebration that my mother's brother is going to hold with his own money. I admire my uncle tremendously. When the day comes, I stand in front of the elders, as calm and collected as a statue, and the audience applauds me. Everyone says that the son of Aliou Sirna Diallo is very tough and brave. After my father hears young girls, women, and men praising my courage, he comes and shakes my hand.

A month goes by and I've completed my initiation. I attain the full status of manhood. From then on, till the day I die, I'll be responsible for my actions, I'll have to face up to the consequences of evil deeds and the benefits of good ones. If I'm honored or dishonored, that's now up to me. My uncle, who knows I don't want to be a shepherd, advises me to become a farmer and promises to buy me the tools I need to till my *guessa* [field]. As an occupation, farming doesn't suit me either, even though I enjoy the sight of ripe millet and corn fields. By this point, my uncle is at his wit's end and he has reached the limit of his generosity and his patience. Since my father can no longer order me to do what he wants, he organizes a council of elders who support his position and make me accept the demands he is making: to stay

---

5. The village of M'Bala was located in the canton (district) of Sovanabé-Botol. A canton was the smallest administrative division of French colonial Africa. Several cantons would be grouped together to form a *cercle* (see n. 1).

with him and be a shepherd for his flocks. Because of the respect
I feel for these elders and for my father's and mother's wishes, I
agree to these conditions and remain a shepherd. Even though my
parents can't legally order me around, I have to respect their age
and remember all the benefits I've received from them.

Winter is coming, it is 1909, and we climb up to the *djeri*
[highlands] where the grass has grown, nature is in bloom, and
it's the pasturing season.[6] We are in Sangom. I take my flocks
out at first light. I'm far from town in the middle of the bush.
Enormous baobab trees with fat green leaves and white, blue, or
reddish flowers look like royalty reigning over all the other trees.
Hypnotized by the beauties of nature, forgetting about my sheep, I
gaze at this sweet-scented land. In truth, only God is able to create
such perfection.

Two gazelles trot by. The noise they make coming through the
fruit trees makes me tremble and my mind races back to my flock.
I look all around but can't see anything except the trees growing
on the immense hillsides. My sheep are gone, lost. I rush to climb
a tree to try to spot them in the distance. Nothing, still nothing.
Clutching my *saourou* in one hand, I run through the forest, climb
the hills, cross over the ravines in a countryside that is sparsely
populated by humans but inhabited by all kinds of animals: lions,
panthers, hyenas, wolves, et cetera.

Night falls. Having seen nothing, I retrace my steps to the village
to find out if perhaps another Fula shepherd, more skilled than
I am, has come across my sheep and brought them back to my
parents. I lie down and look over at our *gallé* [corral]. It's empty.
Because I dread my father's anger, I stay there, away from home, for
two days and three nights. A strange, twisted tree near our straw
hut is my only shelter. I hear the voice of my sister Hava. She calls

---

6. The *djeri* is a dry, sandy area where rains come only in winter.

out: "Bakary Siva Ardé" ["Bakary hasn't arrived home yet"]. And in her voice I hear an emotion that pains me.

The dawn chases away the shadows of the night; the east grows lighter. Worn out from hunger and fatigue, I sleep at the foot of the tree. The flocks amble by as usual, with the cries of shepherds, the murmurs of sheep, the fantastic lowing of cattle. I wake up to see the tall figure of a friend of our family, a Fula man named Gallo. "So, Bakary," he asks, "are you playing the slave here?" I don't answer his question. Instead, I beg him not to say a word to my father and to let me go back into the bush, to die of hunger or get eaten by lions, rather than return to my home village with my *saourou* dishonored. But Gallo insists that I go back to my father with him. "And," he says, "I'll tell him I found you several leagues from here, unconscious under a *baobab* tree." "No, I didn't fall out of that tree. Our beautiful countryside is to blame. Because I was entranced by its marvels, my eyes couldn't stop gazing at it when I should have been watching my flock instead. Tell him that. He'll be more inclined to believe that than if you say I fell. He's passionate about the truth and is also very intuitive, so in a second, he can detect even the most insignificant of lies." Gallo then tells me: "Oh well, if that's what you want, come with me to see your father and we'll tell him everything, together."

I was determined to confront my father's piercing gaze. My own eyes seemed incapable of even seeing what was directly in front of them. As a young Fula, whom the elders know and the young people love, I'm completely tormented by the shame of coming back without my flock, but I don't tremble. Since I had the rank of *gorko* [adult male] bestowed on me a year ago, I'm not afraid, but to tell the truth, I have a mental image of myself standing in front of a crowd of people who are all superior to me and proud of it. Still, I have to go. My conscience is urging me on.

I owe everything to my parents, even my life, so I go back with Gallo, who is worried. He brings me to my father and implores him: "Don't blame him. What happened to him could happen to any Fula herdsman."

My sisters run toward me, looking at me, examining my face. They can see that I'm pale and exhausted. They start to cry and go back to my mother, who refuses to watch what is going on. The pain I am causing my sisters, in particular, becomes even more intense in my heart. My father is clearly shaken by my condition and is kind enough to tell me: "Go, wipe away your tears, eat, get washed, fortify your spirit, and get ready. Tomorrow, early, we'll go together and search for your flock."

Intimidated, disoriented, and especially ashamed of the harm I've done to my family, I become the object of tender care by my mother and sisters. My mother's kindness gives my father an inner strength that I never knew existed before that day. It convinces me that being judged by my father would be my greatest punishment. I think he says to himself: "There's no point in blaming him. He's a worthless *gorko*." This belief, shared perhaps by my friends, especially my childhood friends, overwhelms me and provokes thoughts of suicide. But after more careful reflection, the idea of leaving my mother and my sisters forever makes me see the light in the depths of my soul. My conscience becomes a bedrock of resistance: "I'll live for them."

After my father makes all the necessary arrangements, we leave to search for my flock. When we get to the Védou Kellés [the Lake of the Kellés Trees], the other Fula shepherds greet us courteously but insist they haven't found anything. We keep going along ever lengthening roads, but the gods keep their distance. That morning the sun rises after we do and goes down while we are still trudging on. "This is all my fault," I think. The fatigue, the privations, and all this trouble could have been avoided if I had done my duty as a shepherd. What kind of shepherd am I now? The night, which acts as a shepherd of the trees, hills, and valleys, does not stop us, but it had no voice to tell us where our flock had gone, no information that the trees, hills, or valleys might have given us, if only they could talk! The night is too dark and it's impossible to keep searching. My father says in a tired voice: "Let's go back home."

Hours later we are back in our quiet town. Our friends' flocks, all the people, everything and everyone is asleep. Only my mother and sisters are awake. The fact that we returned empty-handed upsets our loved ones terribly. My father refuses to eat anything but insists that I not follow his example. My sisters urge me to do as he asks, and I eat, but without enjoying the taste of the food.

Months and months go by. It's now 1910. After countless searches, my flock has been found. Two sheep have died, but twenty-five newborns replace them. The rich Fula man who had kept them for a year, this flock that we had no hope of recovering, returns them with these words to my father: "My friend, this kind of bad luck is not so terrible. My only regret comes from imagining how many times you must have searched for them. Today I'm glad to meet another Fula and do him a service. God wanted to see us together on this day and I thank Him for the honor that His mercy has bestowed on me." My father replies in a similar fashion: "My dear friend, you're too kind. I agree with you, and your generosity overwhelms my gratitude."

Now that our flock has come back, my family is happy, but new ideas are bubbling up in my brain, taking the form of painful and irresistible desires. I want to leave Sovanabé-Botol (the region where I was born) and to get as far away as possible. I think: "At Sovanabé, some people care for me, but others don't. The ones who care the most are the young people, especially the young ladies. But youths cannot judge as correctly as the elders. These young people don't really understand why I was such a poor shepherd. As for the elders who criticize my negligence, they only have one line of thinking: 'you are a Fula; therefore, you must, even if you're incapable of it, guard your parents' flock, as all men do.' That's all that they understand. The young people like me, and when they see me, they only think of our childhood games and comradeship." The God of nature is calling me. He wants me to know the wide expanse of the universe. I'll answer his call. I'll leave, yes . . . I'll leave, leaving behind my loved ones and those who welcomed me at Sovanabé.

2.

Toward Ndar[1]

A FTER KISSING MY SISTER MAÏRAM'S HANDS, I LEAVE THE place where I was born, where I know everyone, where everyone knows me, where everyone recognizes me immediately as soon as they see me approaching from afar. I head toward the land of the Wolof which, except for some travelers' tales, is for me a complete mystery.[2] There, no one knows me and I know no one, and yet some magnetic force calls me there, toward the *guédj* [sea]. I arrive in Dagana in January 1911.[3] This is where the prophet Ali Diop died.[4] I have absolutely no money, so I go to the *djama* [mosque] where some devout old men welcome me. They give me something to eat and pray to the Almighty to protect me. I think, "Here are men who love Allah. People say that the Wolofs are very devout, very faithful to the Lord. They have their *djamas* and their Islamic schools, too. This is a land of humane men." I decide to spend the night in the *djéré* [marketplace]; I fall asleep there without a care in the world and have a dream that I'm on a sailboat propelled by a strong wind, where I see some men who say: "There is Ndar."[5]

---

1. The French name for Ndar was Saint-Louis.

2. The Wolof are the largest ethnic group in Senegal. They live in the western half of the country along the Atlantic coast.

3. Dagana, located on the Senegal River, was the provincial capital of the Dagana Circuit.

4. Ali Yoru Diop (1884–1908) was a Muslim holy man who led an armed rebellion against French rule in Senegal. Diop was killed in fighting near Dagana, and his tomb in that town quickly became a pilgrimage site.

5. Saint-Louis (Ndar in Wolof) is located on the Atlantic coast, at the mouth of the Senegal River. It was the capital of French West Africa until 1902, when it was replaced by Dakar. At the time of Diallo's visit, Saint-Louis had about twenty-five thousand inhabitants.

Early in the morning, the sound of the merchants setting up their stalls wakes me, and I walk to the water's edge. At the port of Dagana, the flat-bottomed boats, all lined up in their moorings, catch my eye. I go up to a man who seems to be the guard there and say: "I would like to go to Ndar. Please tell me how I can do that."

"Do you have money to pay for a boat?"

"No, I don't have anything, nothing at all."

"Do you want to work with me on this boat that you see there? It will take you to Saint-Louis in just a few hours."

The prospect of seeing this enchanted city with its beauties and its marvels convinces me to accept his offer and he hires me, telling me that we will leave that evening. I go to see the tomb of Ali Diop and I say my prayers. The clock strikes five, the wind is favorable, and the boat is ready. Its sails are slowly billowing in the breeze. Two *griots*[6] beat their drums vigorously to accompany their songs praising the courage, strength, alertness, and agility of the *laptots* [sailors], while some of us take off our hats to bid farewell to this remote town of Dagana.

As I watch this African spectacle, a flood of thoughts transports me back to my home village, in the district of Sovanabé-Botol. I picture my friends, my comrades, all of my relatives; my overwhelming desire to leave is struggling against the sudden rush of these good and bad memories. I am no longer sure if it is really me who is there among those men who are driven by a passion for *kaliss* [money]. I no longer know if I should return to M'Bala, my village, to remain a Fula shepherd, or if I should stick with my decision to follow my destiny. I'm lost in thought. All of a sudden, my desire turns toward the west. For a short while, I'm overcome

---

6. *Griots* are traditional West African singers and poets who kept alive the important historical memories of their people.

with sadness, and then, happiness returns. I do as the others do; they are singing in the Wolof language—a language that I don't even know.

In the middle of the night, the wind dies and the boat is barely moving. The owner is upset. He tells the sailors to head toward the shore. We take hold of ropes that almost tear through our hands and have to use all our strength to turn the sailboat toward Ndar. Mamadou Seck, the most intrepid among us, has an idea: "Say, Boubakar, you're Fula. Your people, you milk cows, but here we work with ropes, instead. The milk foams depending on the amount of force you use. It's the same thing here, except for the taste. If you pull very hard, we'll see the prow of the boat emerge from the white waves, from the sea foam, like the creamy whiteness of a *calabash* [gourd] full of fresh cream." I listen to him and I understand what he means even though his idea pains me. I pull on the ropes without saying a word. The captain shouts louder; the men who are used to this kind of work double their effort, but I don't know how to go about it. The warm drops of sweat running down my forehead make me take my panther skin handkerchief out of my pocket. Hours and hours go by. Ndar comes into view. It's two o'clock in the afternoon. Some *griots* are singing again; one by one the sailors take their places, directed by the owner. The boat itself seems proud of this dignified arrival. Here we are again landing at Guet Ndar [the port of Saint-Louis].

The incessant movement of white and black people, of wagons and carts, et cetera, in the town, catches my eye, and my mind races. I'm fascinated by all of it. But, I am intensely focused on the question of why the people I see are divided into two groups. They respect each other, and I even think they have a certain amount of empathy for each other. My conclusion is: I guess that what separates them is an imperfect knowledge of their languages.

Sometimes, I suppose, it's also partly a question of skin color. But I can't stop there. I'll have time to think about it more seriously later on. Then, the captain tells us: "You're free until tomorrow morning, till nine o'clock sharp." The sailors change their clothing and go into town, but not me. I can't. I have only one *voutté* [shirt], one pair of pants and *moukés* [shoes]. Nevertheless, I leave the boat and go to the area known as Lodo. My stumbling steps, my wandering eyes, and my ears taking in all the sounds around me make me look like a vagabond who has lost his way. My appearance attracts the attention of passers-by. I understand why a white man close to me says a sentence that ends with the name of my people, Fula. By what sort of magic does he know I'm Fula? My skin is a bit lighter than other blacks, so that might have been a clue. No, he's not possessed by a demon. It's my color, not exactly white but not pure, deep black either, that sets me apart, sadly, in the eyes of whites and black alike. Skin color is the basis of the difference between races.

I come to a bend in a little street. I decide to speak to a big fellow, a Wolof, who seems to be looking at me curiously. I don't speak his language, and he understands only a little of mine. We're both embarrassed, but he walks with me to a café owned by a man named Samba, who's Fula. He treats me almost like a brother. He's kind, polite, and full of charm. He says to me: "My house is your house." His goodness and courtesy exceed all the expectations I had that day.

It's nine o'clock in the morning, the time the owner told us to return. I go back to the boat. Evidently noticing that I'm less sad than I was before, the owner asks me: "Where did you spend the night, little Diallo?"

"In the neighborhood of Lodo, captain."

"You seem happy. What did they do for you?"

"A man took me to the home of another man who received me graciously. That's the reason for my happiness."

The owner thinks and thinks and finally says: "I hope, Bakary, you'll stay with me. Of course, we'll make many trips, but I'll pay you for them."

"Captain, you're kind to want to keep me with you, but I tell you frankly I'd rather stay in Ndar than keep sailing on the sea. I thank you for bringing me here. I'm leaving you with great regret, but I wish you well."

He pulls four silver coins out of his pocket, gives them to me, and wishes me good luck. The sailors come and shake my hand and say: "You should have accepted his offer to stay on board with us, but you're free. Do what you like." When I go back to Samba's café, I meet a young man named Demba Sow. He's a *labbo*.[7] Samba tells us to look for work among the French, so Demba and I both try to follow his good advice. In the center of Ndar, some Frenchmen offer us a job emptying latrines. Since we had no other choice, we accept since it means one franc a day for each of us.

A day goes by. I realize that being a shepherd seems much better than this job. I quit. Demba keeps working and tells me that I'm being unreasonable, that our needs are more important than my feelings of disgust. He tells me I have to ignore them. He's right, but I can't take it any longer. Samba understands me, he feels sorry for me, he commiserates, he gives us some more advice. "You've seen the soldiers going by, haven't you? They come from all races, but the military unites them all. They're the children of the government. They only work when they fight. They're all equal in the eyes of the commanding officer, but any soldier can rise in the ranks if he has the right skills needed. I advise you to enlist tomorrow."

---

7. The *labbo* were a subgroup, or caste, of the Fula people, who were woodworkers and carpenters. The Fula herdsmen, the group from which Diallo came, believed themselves to be a higher caste than the *labbo*.

3.

I Join the French Army

I T'S FEBRUARY 4, 1911. DEMBA AND I ARE STANDING IN FRONT of a handsome black soldier with gold stripes on his sleeve. He's the leader. The other soldiers salute him as they walk by. He raises his right hand with great dignity and spreads his fingers apart—or rather holds his palm facing outward—and returns the salute crisply. Then, he acts as if nothing has happened and turns his attention back to us with a half smile on his face that I am trying to understand. This smile is the kind of twist of the lips that confuses me and I can't figure out what it means since it's neither welcoming nor dismissive. Then I ask him: "How do you like this job? Are you really happy in it?" He answers me with his eyes still on the soldiers leaving the building that he's guarding. His tone is harsh: "You're asking a lot of different things all at the same time. I'll give you one answer for them all: we're not unhappy to be soldiers." Since I keep my eyes fixed on his, perhaps he understands what I want, and he says: "If you want to join up, I'll take you to the office, but I want to make it clear that I'm not advising you to do anything." This he says with a half smile. "You're still entirely free to do as you wish."

"What do you mean, we're still free? Won't we be free after we become soldiers, like you?"

"Well yes, but that depends on how you act," he answers drily.

Demba adds that we already know that. We know that you have to behave correctly everywhere. He's trying to tease the sergeant. I give him a brotherly look and he shuts up. I ask the sergeant to take us to the Recruiting Office. He calls over a soldier who steps up briskly and takes us to the building where the office is located. Now we're inside the office, standing in front of a young white man with a number of gold stripes on his sleeve. He smiles and looks us over with a certain curiosity. He holds a pen in his right hand and it moves smoothly across the pile of documents on his desk. Seeing his handwriting spreading across the paper so quickly makes me want to imitate him. I'm not able to do it at that moment, but "later on I'll learn" is the very powerful feeling I have inside me. The young man hands a document to another soldier and says something to him. Demba and I don't understand anything, but he gestures to us to follow the soldier. He's a black man like us, but he doesn't speak our language, Fula. I decide to ask this man about the rank of the man with many stripes on his sleeve, and our gestures and the direction of our gaze finally make him understand what we want. He tells us, "He's a quartermaster-sergeant." And he adds quickly, "A Frenchman." We appreciate his efforts to explain this to us.

Soon we're inside another building. Our guide explains that this is "Doctor So-and-So." I think that since we're not sick, we don't need to meet the head of the *Lecki* [medical department]. Other soldiers take charge of us and tell us to take off all our clothes. The shame of seeing ourselves totally naked in front of all these people makes me hesitate, but my friend Demba, who's a *labbo*, isn't bothered at all. Everyone's casual attitude upsets me, and Demba, noticing my discomfort, says to me in a low voice: "Bakary, don't be so proud. You know that sometimes we have to adjust to circumstances. A traveler has to be ready for everything and not be surprised by any of it." A thought suddenly strikes me, like a flash of light. I'm more ashamed of getting this advice from a *labbo* than of revealing my naked body, the body of someone who has completed his initiation into manhood [a *gorko*] among the Fula. The world is certainly topsy-turvy. Now the _labbos_ are smarter than the Fula. No, no, and no again. Demba is right. I admire him. Being a shepherd is too confining if we can't get to know other men on a deeper level. But, brought together in different circumstances, on a bigger stage, men can understand each other's true worth. This reassures me and I agree to take off my clothes. The doctor comes in, dressed elegantly. Each of his sleeves has four small gold stripes on it. He talks to us, asking us if we speak Bambara,[1] and finding that we don't, he calls for a soldier who speaks Fula. We have to stand on a scale, get weighed, and measured. Then, the doctor examines us, draping a piece of white linen over our ribs and our chest and asking us to breathe deeply, in and out. He puts his ear to the cloth and listens to our chests. He asks us our ages. I'm eighteen, the interpreter tells him. They estimate Demba's age as twenty-one. When we're finished there, we're brought back to the office of the young white man with gold stripes, the quartermaster-sergeant.

He's still sitting at his desk. I'm still entranced by the way he writes. He fascinates me. His gaze is very calm and seems mild. I examine him with curiosity. He has blond hair, blue eyes, a small straight nose, and a carefully tended, thin mustache. From what I could see of the rest of his body, his neatness is impeccable. When he speaks, the sound of his voice is distinct and natural. There's an undercurrent of laughter beneath his words. When he stops talking, his lips open in a smile. He seems to be a decent man. Demba is silent and motionless, but his eyes, like mine, are taking it all in. No doubt his brain is working. He's definitely thinking. After putting two little books in front of him, the sergeant calls over a black soldier who's standing in the doorway. The soldier steps in smartly, and acting as an interpreter, he asks me for my

---

1. The Bambara are an ethnic group from southern Senegal.

family name, my first name, and my parents' names, as well as my occupation. I'm a shepherd. Demba's a *labbo*. That information is written down and we're taken into a big room, where we're handed over to a short man, a soldier with two red stripes, separated by a black strip of cloth, on his sleeve. This man welcomes us warmly. He speaks Fula and explains to us in these words: "From this day on, you're soldiers. You've agreed to sign up for four years. Until that contract ends, you're required to give complete obedience to the orders your leaders give. In the future, you can become leaders yourselves. That depends on how hard you try. I'm a corporal and my name is Mamadou Racine. I'll treat you well if you're willing to be good soldiers. All the men you see come from different races, but they're not so very different after all because fraternity unites them in town and in the bush."

Soldiers come up to us, shake our hands, and look at our clothes. We chat about this and that, mainly about unimportant things. Demba joins in the talk eagerly. On the other hand, I'm a little shy and reserved, as I've always been. I'm very preoccupied as well. I'm actually thinking of what our friend Samba had said. I still think about it. Life is really strange.

The next day the commanding officer gives an order. We're to go to the parade ground. We do it. There are five of us: three men who signed up the day before us, plus Demba and myself. A "first class" soldier takes us through our paces. He's brisk, very sharp, and really prepared to lead. "Attention!" "At ease." "Attention!" "To the right, right." "To the left, left." "Halt." "Heads high." He approaches us and changes the position of our feet to a wider stance. "Forward, march. One, two, one, two." "Squadron, halt." "At ease." Shouting out the orders isn't hard, but following them correctly is. Nevertheless, almost all of us make some progress. Two days go by. We're issued uniforms and begin weapons training.

"Rifle on the right shoulder." "Put down your rifle." "At ease." And so on.

The soldier drilling us watches us carefully and notices everything we do. He speaks only a little Fula and seems to have difficulty giving instructions in our language, but he's an intelligent man, so he manages. His one mistake is to slap a poor guy who knows nothing about the military but who has come there to learn. That recruit shouldn't have to pay harshly for the errors he's making in drilling. Slaps in the face have never and will never make a good soldier.

A few days later Corporal Mamadou Racine becomes our drill master. Happiness comes to us along with him, and our ability to learn becomes even more obvious. One reason is that the corporal knows how to communicate in Fula with us, and his instructions are crystal clear.

After many, many drills, I'm transferred from the group of new recruits to one made up of more experienced fellows. Demba is kept on with the three others, along with a few new volunteers. This brief separation pains me because Demba is a great friend. We care for each other a lot, like brothers more than like friends. The thought that he's quite intelligent is reassuring. He will be joining me soon enough.

Now I'm with the Wolof who joined up a short time before we did, and even though we don't speak the same language, we manage to make ourselves understood. Some of the men speak Fula and like me, they think the Fula and the Wolof are brothers. I enjoy being with them. The ones who can speak my language also begin to teach me theirs. This interests me greatly and I'm a good student. They say to me, "*Ihoou peulh n'ga*," meaning, "You're Fula." And "*Noun oualoflanou*," which means, "We're Wolof." And "*Peulh ack ouolof benlagnou*," which means "The Fula and the Wolof are one." I'm charmed by their words and begin to love them. The Fula and the Wolof actually should be united, as should all human beings.

We're making progress. Today we study different French sounds. Our leaders' pride in knowing these words inspires them to teach us. Slowly and as seriously as possible, we repeat after them: "Earth, earth; sky, sky," et cetera. Some of us can't say the words correctly, because certain sounds have to be pronounced clearly in order for them to make sense. There's a good reason why the word "sky" (*ciel*) was so hard for us because pronouncing it correctly involves a twisting motion of the tongue. For us, the word "earth" (*terre*) is easier; it has a long sound that is easy to pronounce. We repeat this word in a smooth, even tone. While I'm doing it, my mind probes the word to uncover the how and the why of "earth." I realize that it's a profound question.

The sergeant also teaches us words for family members: "My father, *mon père*, my mother, *mon mère*, my sister, *mon soeur*. But in this lesson, only the name for "father" retains the right gender.[2] At first, it's hard for us to say "*mère*" in the lessons, and yet it's so satisfying to summon her up this way. To say "my father" in Fula is "*Bab-am.*" "My mother" is "*Nén-am.*" Mulling over the differences in speaking these two languages makes my mind wander and I start thinking about the human condition in which we all live, divided, despite ourselves, by the diversity of languages even though language should be a unifying factor. Isn't the essence of human nature, except for skin color, the same in all people? I, Bakary, believe all human nature is the same.

Mamadou Racine takes it upon himself to find a room for Demba and me to rent in town. He finds one and we settle in comfortably.

2. Diallo is referring to the fact that in the pidgin French taught to the African troops, all nouns are masculine. In proper French, the correct form is *ma mère* and *ma soeur*.

The house is about one hundred meters from the barracks and we spend every night there. I know we've got to return to the barracks every morning before six o'clock to be ready for roll call and then either to drill or learn different methods of combat a short distance from Ndar. And, I haven't forgotten our orders to come to the camp at a specific time every morning, but one day I am sleeping more soundly than usual, and this keeps me from waking up at reveille. Instead, I don't get up until around ten o'clock. I start running through the streets of Lodo at top speed toward the barracks wearing only a shirt and underpants; I sprint past people bursting out laughing at the sight of me. I'm carrying my uniform tunic, trousers, and sandals but somehow I lose my trousers and sandals along the way. When I run past the police box, the officer on duty stops me. The chief warrant officer is called and he takes me to the guardhouse, which is dead quiet, even though three other infantrymen are already in detention there. Someone brings me a new pair of trousers and sandals, and so I am back in my military uniform once more. Then, at eleven o'clock the squadrons are assembled to hear the judgment. After the sergeant-major reads it out loud, a Senegalese sergeant, acting as an interpreter, tells me as well as he can in my language: "Bakary Diallo, four days in the guardhouse for missing the morning call and arriving at the barracks at ten o'clock in inappropriate attire." Days go by and I promise myself that I'll be even more vigilant about my behavior. But as luck would have it, I still make mistakes.

I'm a guard at the north gate of the barracks. It's nine o'clock. We have a rule that dogs aren't allowed onto the grounds and the corporal gives me a stick, saying: "This is a direct order. No dog gets in here. Hold this stick and if a dog tries to come inside, your orders are to kill it." "*Mi-nani*, corporal" ["I understand"], I reply. I'm alone at the gate. I look at my stick with such a dreamy gaze

that it seems to transform itself into my shepherd's staff, and at
the end of it I see my flock. Then, this illusion makes me think
I'm still in Sovanabé-Botol. No, it's only my imagination. Despite
the stick in my hand that is the spitting image of my *saourou*, I'm
not a shepherd any longer; I'm a soldier, armed, not with a rifle,
but with a club, ready to grapple with the enemy. But the word
"enemy" makes me pensive and I start speaking in a low voice:
"Poor dog. People say that you're man's best friend. In fact, your
loyalty is unshakable. You're willing to risk losing your life to get
past this gate, simply to be with humans. Why are we chasing you
away? What's wrong with you? What flaws am I overlooking? You
can't give me an answer except through how you look, but I'm
sure if you could express your thoughts, if you could talk, people
would realize how they've treated you with a lack of respect and
gratitude for all the good things you do for them." A few minutes
go by. I stare at the white walls of the base. In my mind's eye I see
the quartermaster-sergeant who signed me up on my first day, the
one who inspired me to imitate him to write as quickly as he did.
With a black pencil in my hand, I trace some lines on the wall. I
do it quickly, but suddenly I hear a loud voice and I look up. It's
the battalion commander. He's walking with his wife and speaking
in French. I don't understand anything that he is saying so he calls
over a corporal to be a translator.

"Why are you writing on the wall?"

"I'm learning how to do it the way the quartermaster-sergeant
who signed me up does it."

"Didn't you see that this wall has just been whitewashed?"

"Yes, that's why it makes such good paper."

"How long have you been in the army?"

"Only a few days."

"Very well. Eight days in the guardhouse for you."

4.

One Morning

I T'S 10:30. THE SOUNDS OF CHIMING CLOCKS AND WATCHES, each with its own timbre, are echoing throughout Ndar, keeping time with the sun's forward march. The sea is the town's inseparable companion, the sound of the waves breaking on the shore seems to reach out to touch the masses of people from all the races of the world there. At the same time, the water is lapping against the boats racing against the handsome *bannit*, Senegal's most admired vessel.[1] People are standing around in many small groups, talking seriously as if they were explaining complex matters. A gentle breeze, warmed by the sun, rustles the *boubous* that the men wear. Women sing lightheartedly, grinding portions of millet in *bobbis* for the midday meal.[2] Children burst out of their houses and run to the sandy playground. They like its smooth surface. Passersby greet each other and shake hands again and again, bringing their hands to their hearts in the Senegalese manner, to show how very much they respect the other fellow. It's a lovely way to express one's feelings, openly and sincerely.

Suddenly, at the base, the trumpeter from the First Infantry Regiment sounds the call to assemble double quick. Only a few minutes later all the infantrymen, even those who were at the other end of town, are gathered at the barracks and the leaders call the roll by company, by section, and by squadron. The

---

1. The *bannit* is a boat used for traveling along the rivers of Senegal. It resembles a large canoe.

2. A *bobbi* is a hollowed-out section of a tree trunk used for grinding ingredients, especially grain.

69

sergeant-majors, with list in hand, stand in front of their units. The commandant and the captains are there, observing it all. We listen to the names being called out, and every infantryman strains his ears to be able to rap out "Present!" My name is called, preceded by my enlistment number: "3003, Bakary Diallo; 3004, Demba Sow; 3005, Fuly Traoré." Once roll call is over, we learn that everyone whose name was called would be leaving for western Morocco in the morning. Looking around, I see nothing but brave reactions from the soldiers. Since they were very young boys, all these young men had been hearing about the great exploits of African warriors like Samba Guéladio Djégui, Samba bo Culatta, Botol Sédi, Al Hadj Umar, and other great men, too.[3] So they're proud to accept the honor that fate offers them, to enter the battlefield and distinguish themselves in the French cause. They're grateful to France for sending them to fight. This, they believe, will help them develop the kind of courage that makes a real man. I hear the men shouting loudly as they handle their weapons, the rifle model 1886. They call it "a true friend," the same way the Bambaras affectionately call the French flag that flies over the entrance to the town, "*Tichébélé*" [the great man]. As for me, I'm already there in spirit. I can see it all in my imagination, but also I'm struck by the changes happening in Ndar, so I keep my thoughts to myself. Imagining all these incredible things makes me feel sleepy. "Come now," I say to myself, "I don't want to be one of those dreamers, those sleepyheads who doze off for no good reason." I reorganize my thoughts and focus my attention entirely on what's happening right in front of my eyes. Since I know nothing about military deployments, I watch the experienced infantrymen and copy what

---

3. Samba Guéladio Djégui was the hero of a West African epic poem, recounting the exploits of a prince, wronged by his uncle, against whom he waged a successful war to regain his throne. Al Hadj Umar Tal (c.1794–1864) was a political leader, Islamic scholar, and military commander who founded an empire over parts of Senegal, Guinea, and Mali. He resisted French incursions into his territory.

they do. I ask them for information, and as they're happy to appear helpful, they give me good advice.

Thanks to them, I'm able to take care of everything I need to do to be ready to leave on time the next morning. First, I hurry to visit a *marabout* named Samba.[4] When I find him right next to the base entrance, on the right, I ask him to make some *gris-gris* [amulets].[5] They cost about forty francs, and Samba promises to have them ready for me by tomorrow. He assures me: "Come early and you'll find them ready to take with you. These holy talismans will protect you from disease and the hail of bullets. I'm sure you'll come back here some day to shake my hand."

The old soldiers look so happy, no doubt reliving wonderful memories from their careers—the remarkable battles they've fought in, their bravery—all of it proof of their loyal service to France. Like men who are determined, no matter what, to defend a master they deem worthy, these soldiers can't wait to get back on the battlefield. Their fighting spirit is clearly visible on their faces, and their happy smiles would make you think that they've already won. Their *coupe-coupe* ["cut-cut," a short saber] gleams in the sunlight and slices through the thick air as they dance. The young infantrymen with only three, four, or six months of service admire the courage their elders are showing, those men who are already seasoned fighters, who have already proved themselves on the battlefield. The soldiers all stand together, ready to emphasize even more vigorously, if possible, how they respond to the call for the ultimate sacrifice from their adopted homeland, France.

It's six in the morning, and I go to see Samba. My *gris-gris* are ready. He takes hold of both my hands and I kneel before him. Then, after blowing three times on my forehead and into my palms, this

---

4. A *marabout* is a Muslim holy man.

5. *Gris-gris* are magical charms that represent a pre-Islamic, African tradition.

mystical holy man says, partly out loud to me and partly to himself, "My child, go where God calls you. He is with you. Be grateful and be sure in your own mind that you know you'll come back to this country." I thank him for his fine words and head to the garrison where my comrades are already standing in formation. I join my unit. The leaders call the roll and the infantrymen answer when their names are called. No one is missing. I see the commandant arrive on horseback. He gives the signal to leave and with the band marching in front, we make our way through town. Our friends from Ndar are standing on the sidewalk, on the right and the left side of the troops, waiting to bid farewell to the men who had been their lodgers and friends. Some of the men's families are walking to the train station, carrying armfuls of little bundles that contain, I'm sure, food for the journey. All of these people make an impressive crowd that catches my attention. I get the impression that we all share the same feelings, feelings that unite our hearts and make us all brothers, brothers on the outside and brothers on the inside.

We climb into the train cars heading for Dakar.[6] The station looks magnificent, decorated in the colors of the French flag. The sky is beautiful and the sun is rising majestically in the splendor of the first morning light. I admire it and call it the prince of all the stars. Civilians bustle to and fro in their colorful clothing. They keep arriving this morning to see the soldiers called to duty on a faraway battlefield in a distant land, but none of the soldiers seem saddened by the inevitable separation that will take place in a half hour. I think they know or believe that war is just a big game in which one simply needs the will to win. With that weighty thought,

---

6. Dakar, a city of around twenty-five thousand people in 1911, had been the capital of French West Africa since 1902. Located on the mid-Atlantic coast of Senegal, it has been Senegal's capital since independence from France in 1960. Its current population is one million.

and convinced, when it comes down to it, that their brothers feel the same way, the civilians don't launch into complicated farewell speeches; they simply say, "See you later." Having seen how calm the townsmen are, I take a look at the women in the crowd. But I don't see the same signs of bravado among them; instead, these sweet creatures look overwhelmed and saddened by this unexpected interruption of the happy life they led with their husbands. I think about my parents and I fantasize about seeing my sisters among the people who have come to see us off. My eyes search this way and that in the crowd, looking for them. I look and look. I even imagine that any minute I will catch sight of them, but "toot, toot" . . . the train leaves, and I haven't seen my sisters Hava or Coumba Diallo. I wanted to see my family, my mother, and my sister Maïram. But didn't the tears flowing from the women's and children's eyes and their gestures calling us back blur my vision?

The train rushes along so quickly that the plains alongside the tracks seem to run in reverse behind all the trees, and the tall *baobabs* that tower over everything else look like they're charging with fixed bayonets. I enjoy watching the trees racing along to meet the train that's carrying us to Dakar. The scene looks like a battle plan. My soldier's brain imagines that the trees represent the enemies waiting for us in Morocco and that we soldiers are the moving train. The trees are stationary, rooted in the ground, so they can't run away from the impact of our iron fist that keeps coming at them. Downed branches are the wounded fighters, and felled trees are the dead. The screeching noise of the train becomes the victorious charge of we Senegalese infantrymen, and the plumes of smoke bellowing from the engine are the fire of our relentless weapons. I suddenly catch sight of a wolf 250 meters from the train tracks. He looks terrified and I keep staring at his head poking up from the ground, imagining him howling with fear. My word, I pitied that poor devil, all alone in the summer bush. Demba Sow pulls me away from the train window, saying, "You look sad, Bakary. Are you still with us?" "I was thinking of that little wolf we saw a few minutes ago." And I add, since I wanted to keep talking, "And then . . ." But Demba looks at me and quickly interrupts me, "You're daydreaming, just as if you were asleep. Ever since I met you, I've seen you dreaming as if your thoughts were the only food that sustains you." Demba's observation strikes me. He's right and I tell him so, asking him to forgive me for being lost in thought so often. I also admitted that I can't help myself. "Me too, I'm a thinker," he says. "But," he adds forcefully, perhaps convinced that I had drifted off into dreams again, "I don't keep thinking to the point of lulling myself to sleep." "So, are you satisfied with that, Demba?" He replies, "For myself, yes . . . But you, I think you'll be locked in eternal combat with your imagination." "Listen, Demba, we're all alike. No one thinks more than anyone else. You've noticed my dreamy state because your mind is always alert. The only real difference between people's minds is the direction their thoughts will take. Everyone's mind is made for a special purpose, a unique one, though we all have the ability to consider anything and everything, an unlimited number of things. I can assure you that even though I'm quiet when I'm caught up in my thoughts, I'm nevertheless thinking and caring about you." My good friend Demba fixes his big eyes on me. I have the impression he wants to say something, but all he does is look at me.

At last we arrive in Dakar. My impression of this city that I'm seeing for the first time is not negative, not at all. We're directed to the barracks, where, it seems, we're going to stay for a few days. It is May 2, 1911, and the battalion is ready to board the boat leaving for Casablanca, Morocco. The band from the General Government of French West Africa, which veterans can't stop praising, marches in front of the departing troops. Cheered on by the residents of Dakar, the infantrymen are ramrod straight in their spotless army gear, and attract admiring looks from everyone, even the littlest children, who are pulled along in the parade's wake by some mysterious patriotic force. It's wonderful to see everyone walking toward the port with this intense enthusiasm. No tears, no sobs, one would think it's a pilgrimage to a holy place. The troops halt and line up before the boat with the French tricolored flag. "Present arms!" A government official reviews the troops as they march by. It's the governor-general of French West Africa.[7] Once the inspection is over, the troops get on board. I take a look at the naval officers. They are superb in their black dolmans and they look like good leaders as well. After we take our places, I begin admiring this stupendous ship, bigger than any I've ever seen. Then, the boat whistle sounds three times, sharply, like a big angry elephant, and the vessel gets underway. People on the shore wave their handkerchiefs as they watch us leave, and our handkerchiefs wave back. I compare their varied colors to people's skin. I mean (forgive me for this comparison) their handkerchiefs seem to correspond to the skin tones of all the people gathered there. All the colors of humanity are present on that day: pure white, pure black, partly white, partly black, yellow, and others that I can't quite make out.

The excitement is infectious. We see it in the looks on the faces of the men who are leaving, crossing the sea to another shore. The boat picks up speed, gradually leaving the port behind. We can still see Dakar; some of the taller buildings stand out, then only the telegraph poles.[8] Finally, it all disappears from view. Nightfall intensifies the distance between us and the Senegalese coast, our

7. At this time, the governor-general was Amédée William Merlaud-Ponty, who served from 1908 to 1915.

8. Diallo is referring to the TSF (*telegraphie sans fil*), the "wireless telegraph," or radio, used to communicate with ships at sea.

homeland. Darkness spreads across the sky, enveloping everything, even the sea where the waves are rumbling loudly. I can see nothing in the distance but I keep on hearing the powerful thunk of the waves. I think about going to sleep. My eyelids are heavy and I guide myself to my assigned berth by instinct. Stretched out on the quilt I use for a bed, I await the mysterious balm of sleep to calm my senses, despite the rocking of the ship.

I open my eyes when someone grabs my arm. It's Demba. "Good morning, Sow," I say, shaking his hand. "Good morning, Diallo, get up, it's time for coffee. Did you sleep well, my friend?" I tell him I couldn't complain about our night on the water. "And you, Demba?" "Thank God," he replies, "I've been spared seasickness till now and I hope for all of our sakes that I stay that way." We drink our coffee and I ask Demba to come with me to the bridge. He says yes immediately and off we go to look at the water. Our eyes search in vain for the sight of land. In the distance, the sea is tinted a brilliant white where the magnificent sun is rising, and it's more impressive than ever. Some white birds with patches of gray and blue are wheeling and diving near the boat, as if to tease this behemoth or to figure out what this whale really is. Their beating wings remind me of the handkerchiefs fluttering their farewells in the port of Dakar. My whole body shivers and my mind sends a message by some sort of mysterious telepathy to all my loved ones in Senegal. My parents appear before me and I gaze at them, remembering how much they care for me, a love that began with my first sight of the world. Demba, who sees that I'm absorbed in thought, gives me a friendly tap on the shoulder. "Stop that!" I'm afraid . . . no, I'm troubled by his cries, and I ask my kind friend what I'm supposed to stop. "Your thoughts," he replies simply. Then I say, "Is it possible, my faithful guardian, to stop my thoughts once they're set in motion?" "No," he replies, "but all the same, it seems to me to be only reasonable to control the thoughts that we have when we're awake." "Precisely, Demba. That's why I'm sometimes lost in thought: when the ideas come to me, on no matter what subject, I try to figure out their significance, without rushing things in any way, and that's why I seem to you to be a perpetual daydreamer." "Then," Demba says, "I'm sorry that you don't know how to read and write, either in Senegalese or in French, because then you could put your thoughts on paper since they're worthwhile for everyone to know. If I knew how to read and write, I would be your secretary, but my God! I don't know any more than you do." "Demba, do you remember why I was disciplined at Ndar, when I was guarding the northern gate of the garrison of the First Senegalese Battalion, when I wanted to write with a black marker on the newly whitewashed walls? I decided then that I wanted to learn French and that I had to be able to write, read, and speak this language that our white officers speak. I already know a few words: "Me happy to drink some awter (water) . . . Me ask bermission (permission) . . . Me leave for town . . ."[9] Demba repeats after me. He wants to learn, too. It's time to eat and a bell summons us to the mess hall. We obey and "*lana inaï yadé*" [the boat keeps sailing]. After lunch, my head is spinning and I feel nauseous. I'm suffering from seasickness. I throw up everything I've just eaten. I go back to my bunk and lie down, and Demba takes such good care of me, demonstrating his comradeship, his friendship, and his very sincere affection.

---

9. Here, as elsewhere in the book, Diallo is trying to convey his imperfect grasp of French, before he became more fluent in the language.

5.

On the March

THE NEWS SPREADS: "LAND HO!" THE UNIT LEADERS START getting the troops ready. I get up, still feeling very weak, like many others who can barely move a muscle. I look at Demba and he nods at me with a gesture that I understand as meaning, "In any case, we're getting off soon. That's not bad." At that moment, the boat whistle blows and we all shout with joy. The boat comes to a halt. We're there. The troops disembark under the watchful eyes of all the top brass in Casablanca. It's the first time I've seen so many officers from so many ranks: the infantry, artillery, general staff, and quartermasters. There are also some officers with white stripes on their uniforms, whose significance I don't yet understand. People say they're veterinarians. A band plays the stirring melody of "La Marseillaise" and the echoes of the song seem to penetrate deep into the sea.[1] You might say that it wants to go where we had begun our journey five days ago, and follow its traces, now disappearing beneath the waves. But no, that isn't the case. Maybe I'm mistaken because we were all listening to the song. We love it and we listen so closely that it envelops us. It attracts us the way a snake hypnotizes a bird. We're searching for the traces of great French soldiers, whether they're black or white, in "La Marseillaise," and we'll keep looking for them, if necessary, till the day we die.

The troops set off, heading northwest from the town. Halt . . . This is it, the place to make our bivouac. It's hard to see anything

---

1. "La Marseillaise", the French national anthem, celebrated the military exploits of the Revolution of 1789, which overthrew the monarchy.

clearly in the dark night. Still, we have to cook the evening meal. The guards are at their posts, and I'm on guard duty with the rest of the squadron led by my corporal, Sylleyman-Sidibé. Our orders are: "Don't let anyone into the camp without the password. The guard will call out 'Halt!' three times. If the intruder doesn't stop, you must fire on him and hit him. Don't miss!" "I've got it, corporal, and I hope my two hours will go by without having to do that." "Yes, but you must be extra alert. We're not in Senegal any more. You're in Morocco, you realize that, Bakary, don't you?" "Yes, corporal, I do. I'll pay even more attention." I am standing facing the sea. I keep watch and nothing distracts me from my duty. When my time on guard duty is over, Demba comes to relieve me. I tell him the orders and the password. "Don't worry, Bakary," he replies with a smile. "I'm on duty tonight, my eyes are sharp, and I pity the guy in the sights of my rifle." I go back to our camp. It's only ten o'clock. I see that Demba has fetched water for himself and for me, so I shave and lie down to get a little sleep.

The trumpet plays reveille. I haven't gotten enough sleep. My weary eyes want to close again, but I do everything in my power to keep them open. I get ready quickly, putting on my gear and finishing my morning coffee before the morning drill. Hours go by and it's mealtime again. Moroccans gather all around our camp with all kinds of things for sale. They nibble on pastries made of corn, barley, wheat, and honey and look a bit timid and fearful, but still motivated by the prospect of earning some *souldis* [Moroccan money]. They're also selling oranges. At first glance, I prefer the oranges, simply because I don't know how clean their kitchens are. The pastries aren't very appealing to men whose stomachs are full, but the oranges are excellent. The vendors want to know how long we'll stay, no doubt in order to find other ways to make money, but we soldiers "don't know nuthin' . . ." Certainly, we'll be leaving for Rabat soon, but during wartime, "no say much . . ."

It's a beautiful day when we hear the assembly call. There are no clouds overhead, just a clear blue sky. It seems the heavens want to reward the eyes that are contemplating its divine clarity. The officers standing near the commandant gather around to hear the order for our march to Rabat. On the sea, steamboats whistle as if they're saluting our departure and want to bid us farewell. The town is quiet, but it seems unhappy; it smokes so much. The forward squadron and the side squadrons take up their assigned positions. The trumpet blares and the troops begin moving. We cross a countryside dotted with hills and valleys. We see wheat and barley, already ready for harvesting. The first planting is ripe. It's impressive to see these places that we'd never seen before. My eyes catch sight of many different kinds of trees and I can recognize fig trees and plum trees among them. The farmers, however, have left their fields and are hiding in "casbahs,"[2] staying out of sight because we, the military, have arrived. I feel sorry for these poor guys, forced to abandon the primary responsibility of their lives, but I comfort myself knowing that we'll soon be far away from their fields, and then they'll come back.

Reveille is played as usual. We get ready to leave early in the morning. Forward march! Our column advances in combat formation on the road toward our destination. Still the same fields, the same lovely views, and always empty of human life. The soldiers are lighthearted, singing African songs and doing their favorite dances as we march along. Our high spirits infect even the worst laggards. We take breaks every ten minutes to let everyone rest a bit and enable the slowest ones to catch up. We can see Rabat in the distance. That makes us happy because we know we'll make camp in a little while. The order comes and we stop on the outskirts of town in front of a mill that looks like a well. I see two horses harnessed in a haphazard fashion to two long yokes, walking in a circle as if they've

---

2. Casbahs are fortresses or citadels in North Africa.

become accustomed to it and have no hope of ever stopping. As they walk, always at the same pace, clear water flows from the water mill. The animals are mute, they keep pulling and pulling, like slaves condemned to eternal punishment because they had disobeyed an order. The horses don't even notice the troops assembled before their eyes. I call out to Demba, I pull him next to me, and I point out to him the horses that power the mill. I say to him: "The sight of these creatures, which we call animals, upsets me greatly because they can't express themselves. They can't tell us, the creatures we call humans, what they're thinking. Just seeing them like this really makes me realize that there must be many things in their minds that we ought to know about in order to alleviate their suffering. Unfortunately, humans believe that animals are created just to serve them and obey their will." "Come, come, Bakary," Demba says, "you have pity for so many things. What can you do about the muteness of these poor creatures? What can you do about the profits men get from their labor? Nothing, you can do nothing. Even if animals could talk, men wouldn't pity them since their powers are so unequal, and if animals aren't men's equals, they'll always be subservient. Self-interest comes first, doesn't it, Boubakar?"

"Of course, Demba, I myself know that men are terribly attached to what they call 'interest' because life teaches us that lesson, but really, what shocks me is that this lesson hasn't encouraged men to take better care of the needs of those who are most useful to us. Man doesn't come into the world smarter than an animal who is older than he is, but because humans can express themselves, their needs are served so that they will keep quiet about the evil they see. On the other hand, we constantly let animals witness so many stupidities that are as awful as the injustices we inflict upon them, on the pathetic pretext that 'it's just an animal, it won't say anything.' Come on, Demba, are we right to treat animals that way, creatures that are so useful for us?" "I understand. We shouldn't act this way. We're all put on this earth to help each other. But, don't you see, Bakary, life is really just a cloth made of many different threads. Every creature is destined by our Creator to play the part assigned to him, and once that is done, he gives way to a new creature, and on and on. At least that's the way it's been for a long, long time. No one can deny the idea that one day those poor downtrodden beings that you pity will become our masters, and our superior status today will come to an end." I look hard at my loyal friend Demba, hoping he had more to say, but he seems plunged in thought and naturally I can't disturb him. As we leave, I look back at the two horses, who haven't stopped working, not even for one second. You poor devils, may new miracles of fate come to your aid! May your masters appreciate your merits and fulfill your desires!

The troops go through the town and stop on the banks of a fairly wide river they want to cross. Moroccan flat-bottomed barges are quickly requisitioned. The soldiers go across unit by unit and set up camp on a wide stretch of the grayish-yellow sand that lines both banks of the Rabat River. Night has already fallen, obscuring our view. The fatigue of the long march helps to lull the soldiers peacefully to sleep, except for our courageous sentinels. We sleep as calmly as if the city nearby were only occupied by Frenchmen. But we're roused abruptly, ready to fight, but then we hear that this is a false alarm caused by one of the sentinels posted on the eastern perimeter who had fired his rifle for no reason. We creep back into our tents and even have to put some of them back up because they had fallen down during the alarm. Infantrymen with a sense of humor say, laughing, that the poor sentinel had not shined on this dark night. Mamadou Ba adds: "The guard thought the 'tooth' of his rifle could bite the shadow of a tree in front of it.[3] Luckily, the tooth heard all the troops coming to its aid. Otherwise, it might have kept firing till the shadow was declared innocent by the dawn and the fading away of the night." I'm kept awake by my Senegalese comrades' talk, since they couldn't see why a soldier would have acted that way.

Then, we're on the march again. Bursting with high spirits, we sing all kinds of songs. The different nations in our unit keep up their spirits with beloved *djimis* [songs] from their own land. The Bambaras sing out with gusto: "*Badialamamé ah . . . vadialama tienjio badialamama kelé nié.*" The Wolofs sing: "*N'Daga Diaye y allah bomerere y allah bodem ourianne, alli seynabou.*"[4] And the soldiers from other countries—French Guinea, Dahomey, Ivory Coast—sing just as lustily.[5] They seem to find a special meaning in every word, uncovering fascinating insights from the storehouse of ideas, from our most ancient myths, from the very beginning of the world. It's enough to make your head spin: tales of ancient black warriors whose deeds live on in our heritage, not in printed books, but in the lands where these exploits take place. The memories live on, stored intact in every newborn child's brain. Despite the diversity of nations, of songs, of thoughts, of tastes, nothing that I could see reveals what people call "difference," not even on the most superficial level. You could even say that everything we do is meant to unite us. I mean, the songs we sang on the road that day were ones that each of us understood as an *expression* of the goodness and nobility that makes all men brothers. We arrive at Sidi Guedarr where the farmland is particularly good for cultivating oats and barley. A superior officer orders the men not to damage this natural

---

3. The "tooth" is understood here to be the bullet, which is "inside" the rifle. "Tooth" (*dent* in French) sounds like "inside" (*dans*), so the sentinel's mistake becomes the butt of jokes by his fellow soldiers.

4. "*N'Daga Diaye*, if God is not angry with you, may you not go to Ourianne."

5. These different nations were all part of the vast colony of French West Africa.

bounty, and it's an order that the Senegalese infantrymen follow
with special pleasure because they consider it very important; this
is a command that shouldn't be ignored. As for me, it makes me
especially glad because the stewardship of that harvest deserves
the greatest respect. One by one, the farmers start coming out
of hiding. They seem to be afraid to show themselves in the fields
where we are setting up camp but at the same time, they are also
eager to make sure that nothing is destroyed. It's sad to see their
anxiety, knowing in our heart of hearts that we have no ill intentions
toward them. But this kind of thing drives away human kindness.
Instead, ignorance holds sway because if God had given humans
the ability to empathize with other people's true feelings instead
of having to rely on assumptions, so much pain and unhappiness
could have been avoided, no matter how wide the gulf between
us, especially in circumstances like these. Fortunately, in this case
our French commanders know how to break through the fog of
misunderstandings that keep the soldiers and these farmers apart,
that wound men's hearts and distract their minds.

We'll spend a few days at Sidi Guedarr to perform reconnaissance
in the area. A group of Moroccan fighters came and rained bullets
on our encampment. I believe one horse was wounded and two
killed, but we barely caught sight of our attackers. They fled like
rabbits into the vast mountain range to the east. Night falls, and it's
time for dinner. A Foreign Legionnaire, who came to spend some
time with our unit, says jokingly: "Tonight we're going to eat the
horses that were killed." The Senegalese who hear this nonsense
refuse to eat. The unit leaders, Europeans and Africans, try in
vain to debunk it but it's impossible, and the infantrymen who are
devout refuse to eat the food.[6] And it's pointless to try to change
the mind of someone who is absolutely convinced otherwise.

---

6. In Islam, horsemeat, like pork, is considered unclean and cannot be eaten by
observant Muslims.

6.
Through the Mountains

THERE ARE VERY HIGH MOUNTAINS BETWEEN SIDI GUEDARR and Mecknès. We cross them on foot the way monkeys climb trees, but our vehicles—supply wagons, ambulances, and cannons—struggle on the journey. Both ways—going uphill and back down the other side—are equally difficult. We climb up with our heads tilted backward and go down crouching forward with our chins touching our knees. Given this situation, we soldiers first have to reach the mountain top on foot, then put our packs down and go back to get the wagons waiting at the foot of an amazing jumble of rocks. We have to ford a river without taking off our shoes, and then our feet are trapped inside shoes that are shrinking as they dry. It's painful and some soldiers lag behind as much as a few hundred meters. Some even collapse on the ground, unable to move any further. That's when the squadron leader proves his mettle, and that's how the ordinary foot soldier punishes his corporal. The corporals have to carry the laggards' packs. And that's also when, in order to reward them, the corporals carefully note which soldiers marched well and helped them accomplish this difficult task. It's an intense struggle, engaging every part of the body from head to toe, from mind to heart, from soul to conscience.

I'm on guard duty at the foot of an isolated tree, and that reminds me of the day when Gallo found me huddled at the foot of a tree at home. But at that time, I was the shepherd for a flock of sheep; now I'm still a shepherd, but of men who know how to shape their own destinies in this world. This is what fate is: a force driven by an unknown power puts all living beings somewhere in the world, and when we bow to the will of this mysterious entity, we fulfill our destiny. We arrive at an orchard planted with olive trees. It's a small field to the northeast of the town, just at the beginning of the road to Fez. A Moroccan market springs up very close to us and the merchants hawk local produce: figs, melons, plums, and tea—these are the goods the Senegalese prefer. I want to find out what these men think about us. How can I go about it? Can I really understand the deepest feelings of people I only see for ten minutes a day and whose language I don't even speak? Will I be able to recognize the instinctive gestures they make that would bring mutual understanding to their hearts and mine? What part of the body will reveal those movements, those truly blessed signals of the human spirit? I search for an answer . . .

I see two tents side by side. One looks neater and cleaner than the other. Since, in spiritual matters, cleanliness is essential for truth, I decide to chat with the proprietor of the cleaner tent first before I visit the humble owner of the second one. Standing face-to-face with this man with bronze skin, black eyes, and black hair, I search for something to buy in order to start a conversation: a cup of tea. I point to the steaming teapot. No doubt, in order to make sure he understands my order, the owner picks up a metal cup, brings it up to the teapot, and with his other hand, holds a gold-plated spoon that stops the flow of the steam, skillfully, like someone who wants to avoid getting scalded. He looks at me quizzically, wanting to be sure that I want the tea. His face suddenly clears. He beams with a smile whose sincerity convinces me. I ask him if he speaks French or Senegalese. He shakes his head no, moving it from left to right, and sad thoughts take hold of my mind. I glance down at the ground without actually seeing it. My God! I think of all the evil that arises and flourishes in ignorance. Human hearts come together, beating in unison, with the same feelings.

Humanity, that's the right word. But there are different countries, races, and colors mainly because the world, so amazing, is also so vast. This gives rise to divisions, and thus, different languages that cause damaging misunderstandings between human beings.

How wonderful it would be to hear the clarity of a universal language that everyone could use.[1] People suffer so much because they don't understand each other. What causes quarrels and wars based on so little, if not misunderstandings? Every injury springs from incomprehension, and every good comes from an evil that is clearly understood. My God! What is the solution? This is the source of all human suffering. It spreads among us like the fog drifting across the Sahara. Each man has his heart hardened by ignorance, his soul diverted, misled, frightened, emptied of virtues, and overcome by illusions. We should applaud the men and women who are working to establish the principle of world peace. Attaining this dream can only happen if we develop the natural tendencies of newborn souls; here I mean children as soon as they begin to mimic adults' gestures and actions. All children come into the world with a temperament consisting of equal measures of goodness and virtue. They are clean slates and know nothing of the layers of dirt that will soil them to a greater or lesser extent, depending on their upbringing. It is absolutely true that dirty linen can be washed clean when there is soap, but the precondition for virtue in humans is that there must be absolute cleanliness. It is a thousand times better not to be soiled to begin with. Standing in front of the Moroccan men's tents, I ask myself: What would be the point of going to the next man to pursue my simple investigation? That man I just left: Hasn't he revealed enough to my heart and mind?

---

1. Diallo's longing for a "universal language," found expression in the contemporary Esperanto movement. Esperanto was created in 1887 by Polish physician L. L. Zamenhof as a universal language to foster peace and international understanding.

We have to move on. There's a rebellious pocket north of Mecknès, an uprising against the occupation in a place that doesn't recognize the generosity of the French. We cross a river between two small hills and head toward the high mountains where Moroccan insurgents have set up camps. It's four o'clock in the afternoon. A distant sound reaches us. It's our adversary's forward sentinels who are sounding the alert about our presence. We hear other shouts, followed by rifle fire: "Kao . . . Kraou . . . Kraou . . ." The sun is setting. In a few short moments, souls will leave this night to take refuge in the other. What I imagine is going to happen sends shivers throughout my body, but I take care not to let anyone see it, not even Demba to whom I have already confided so many things. This is because our soldiers prize courage in battle above all else. If the others, by some misfortune, notice me trembling with fear, I'll lose their respect forever. "Low morale" will be their verdict because they often say: "We must not fear death when everything is in God's hands." So, honestly, even though my heart is fluttering inside my chest, on the outside, I feel myself girded in iron. The attack is inevitable. The alarm sounds. We take up arms. The Moroccans attack as if they mean to overrun our camp. Our commanding officers order us to close ranks. Captain Coste, our leader, gripping his revolver in one hand and his saber in the other, leads us quickly onto the mountain to the west. Bullets are raining down on us. But the Moroccans see us approaching with fixed bayonets. They retreat and flee down a steep ravine. Captain Coste, lying on his back, his legs in the air, sings French songs to himself. It looks as if he was simply relaxing in the moonlight. I couldn't believe a white man could be so brave, but suddenly he stands up and charges to the right. Six armed rebels appear before us, their white burnooses fastened with red rope, hiked up around their waists. The captain had spotted them before any of us infantrymen stretched out on the ground on our bellies.

He raps out an order: "Ready, fire!" But these six pilgrims don't wait for our bullets to fly. They disappear into the ravine. Our company commander can't help laughing when he sees this hasty retreat. "It really wasn't worth their coming to take a look at us," he says, glancing at his sword. Then, the battle gets more intense. Captain Coste, who only has one squadron with him, wants to take stock of his men's positions since they're scattered over this vast terrain. He beckons to a European sergeant from our section and asks him to designate two volunteers to go with him to find the second, third, and fourth sections that are spread out on the mountain. I quickly run to his side along with Moussa Konaté. The captain gives us a piercing look with his big black eyes and says: "Let's go. Follow me." We follow his every step. He walks with no hesitation, holding his revolver in his hand, ready to shoot. Bullets fly toward us from every side because our position is surrounded, but the captain stands up straight as if he wants to be as high as the bullets that whiz by our heads like bees buzzing around flowers. The captain almost falls down a ravine but is quickly grabbed by a hand. He turns around to say: "Ah . . . thank you, Bakary." Then we come to a camp which is almost deserted. Since the captain doesn't see anything there, he heads toward a ridge on the northwest, and there we find the other sections. Our mission is accomplished and the captain shows his gratitude by saying: "Good soldiers, thanks."

7.

Conversations before Fez

W E'VE BEEN BIVOUACKING NEAR FEZ FOR SIX DAYS. Demba Sow is looking for me and so I join my dear friend. "Hello Demba, how are you feeling?" "I'm fine. Thanks, Bakary. And how are you?" "How I feel, my dear Demba, depends. I can compare my feelings to a chameleon that changes color according to where it is. If I'm near righteous things, I feel fine, but I can hardly stand to see peaceful relations between people in jeopardy. That is precisely when goodness is most necessary. Even though I am obligated, in any case, to do my duty, I absolutely have to focus on positive thoughts when I think about humanity. This is because, my dear friend Demba, every human being is bound to look for causes and effects in everything that happens. We do this in order to know how much of it is true. I don't understand why there are misunderstandings between people who all consider themselves to be enlightened. Every man, from the day he is born, is endowed with enough reason to ensure that essential character traits are not betrayed. The main thing is to avoid pridefulness, vanity, and indifference in human relations, and inattention when we are listening to someone else speaking. What's the point, my friend, of trying to pretend to be superior to one's neighbor since we are all made the same? When we share our knowledge with others only in order to show off, to make them think we're more intelligent than they are, we are actually demeaning ourselves. Honestly, Demba, since we all love peace and quiet, I don't see what motivates men to be violent toward one another. Diseases and death are part of nature, but except for those, my friend, do you think there should be any reason for people's unhappiness?"

Demba looks up at the sky with his eyes wide and replies: "I understand everything you've said. I agree with you about brotherhood. Mental suffering is absolutely avoidable. Everyone wants to live well, both mentally and physically. Adults, I mean grown-ups, were so tiny at birth that their fathers and mothers had a sacred duty to do their best raising them. Parents sacrificed for their children, who flourished because of this care motivated by tenderness and love. But we remain children, even when we're grown, because there are always other people bigger than we are. Like children who depend on their fathers and mothers, we need help throughout our lives, and we must also help others. We have to love helping others as much as we love life itself. True happiness is based on respect and affection and is reinforced when we help each other. Sowing and reaping: one never happens without the other." He continued: "You asked me to speak, my dear Bakary, but did you expect to hear what I just told you? In everything that our hearts and minds show us, what can we make better? We freely discuss our ideas but we are too little compared to the real problems of life. Admit it, Bakary, we are like birds whose wings have lost their feathers. That's why I tell you this again: Think less, a lot less, if you don't want to remain a permanent and tormented student."

When Demba says the word "tormented," he stops looking at me as he usually does. He shifts his gaze to a Senegalese sergeant who is organizing a work party of infantrymen to haul supplies. My affection for him brings my hand up to rest on my friend's right shoulder. Demba turns to face me, smiling. He tells me, "I'm watching Sergeant Fofana with his duty squadron." I reply: "Yes, and you must think that this handful of men will really help us achieve the clarity we're after. They're going out to gather food for the troops. They're going to revive our tired bodies, exhausted from the long march, and help us get in shape for tomorrow's deployment. At dawn tomorrow the locals will get a look at the troops of Glorious France. They'll see that we are the sons of dynamic, intelligent, good, and capable people. They'll admire our immense power as we march under the French flag. Their admiration and their logic will help them understand the real basis for the French mission. They will become like us. From now on, this opportunity is theirs for the taking. To be involved with the French is to learn to love what they love. The Senegalese have really been transformed. Their ideas, their tastes, the way they act, the desires and pleasures that they kept alive and passed down from generation to generation couldn't resist French ways. It isn't that our customs aren't proper, not at all, but we really ought to acknowledge a certain finesse in the French approach. It's precisely this sophistication the Moroccans will notice first when they watch us in action. France is used to impeccable behavior, and we, who come here to fulfill France's duty to humanity, will certainly take care to uphold all her traditions. The Moroccans simply must recognize the great benefit being offered to them." Demba agrees with me on this point. He says that France deserves its reputation and he remarks in all seriousness: "Bakary, since I've been spending time with you, I've begun to think more than I used to. I can see the different truths of many things and, certainly, with such a capable nation, we can do a lot of good." Demba stands up. He's heading to his squadron's tent, a few steps away from ours, to sleep. While shaking my hand, he says, "*M'Balen e Diam*" ["Sleep in peace"]. I get up to walk with him for a bit. The hand I'm shaking conveys the great sincerity of his heart. "Good night, my friend," I tell him.

Our enemies' attacks are getting weaker. Things are settling down, a sign of peace. Are the rebels lucky enough to realize that it's better not to fight against France? We infantrymen often talk about the advantages for these people if they surrender. It's true. France's power is so vast that it could protect all of Africa. France has a noble heart and a spirit of absolute fairness. That's why it's been given a mission of utmost importance, to ensure good relations and understanding among people. Ousmane Demba Diallo, a fellow soldier, said one day, "A Frenchman's face is so open, honest, and kind that, for my part, I have always liked it." I feel the same way, and in truth, any right-thinking person would come to the same conclusion as Ousmane does about a real Frenchman. Ousmane had told me this one bright moonlit evening when I asked him what he thought of the French. Standing with fifteen other black soldiers, Ousmane said: "You're asking me that, Bakary? Well, just between ourselves here, all of us black men, I'll let my conscience be my guide in the answer I must give you." And Ousmane did just that, sincerely, and all the comrades there agreed with him, except for Yero Ba. He said, "I don't think that way at all. The French are too arrogant. They think they're better than everyone else." But Alassane Dicko, almost losing his temper, turned to Yero and asked excitedly: "You don't want to agree with the rest of us? Ah! Yero, aren't you forgetting something? Haven't you thought about the awful things the French banished from our country when they came? The people whose lives were saved by those brave men won't say the same as you. The villages always being torched, the flocks stolen with no regard for their owners, thousands of harvests carried off by warriors who slaughtered everything they laid eyes on, women separated from their children, old people robbed and sometimes even killed. If they could speak, they wouldn't talk like you. Don't you know anything about this, Yero? It's obvious you don't know much about history.

Bakary Diallo should add a few words to clear up your mistaken ideas. I'm sure he doesn't agree with you." Actually, while Alassane Dicko was speaking, I imagined scenes of looting, robberies, men fighting wars, wars between countrymen of the same race, and men on horseback menacing flocks. Above all, I saw mothers torn from their children who were crying, slaves tied to horses' tails, forced to walk for vast distances, children frozen with fear when they saw, not their beloved mothers coming, but men armed to the teeth, ready to massacre everything in their path. And the little ones who were still calling for "papa . . . mama . . ." With all that in my mind's eye, I couldn't keep myself from exclaiming: "The truth, my friends, is in things that none of us actually witnessed, but we can well imagine the most horrific sights. The history of our country commemorates important events of the past, and if we compare our history before France came with the history after, up until now, then we'll have nothing but well-deserved gratitude for the French. We ought to be grateful for our parents' sake and our own that we are serving France and working under her leadership to unite all the world's peoples. In all seriousness, we have an opportunity to acquire her knowledge and to adopt her way of life. Let's show France our true thoughts and feelings in good conscience. Let's love her as we love ourselves, and then we'll see her heart, her soul, and her mind open up to teach us with the best will in the world."

8.

In the Infantrymen's Camp

W E'VE BEEN BACK IN FEZ FOR SEVERAL DAYS WHEN WE are joined by the soldiers' wives.[1] The Senegalese women are glad to see their husbands again, and they show it, bringing us coffee flavored with sugar and spices and the homemade sweets they had prepared as a special treat. The single men can't help but be happy too because the wives and husbands invite them to join in their celebrations. We all depend on the soldiers' wives' hospitality. These women are accustomed to army life so that, even in the harshest circumstances, they can tolerate hunger, thirst, and all kinds of hardships. They're ready to support their husbands with the utmost devotion and courage. You might assume, at first, that women like these had lost their feminine sensitivity, but the depth of their unquestioning obedience to their husbands and their profound love for them and their children is unimaginable. Then again, why and how should these women's courage surprise us? They certainly don't lack experience with romantic love or human intelligence, but first and foremost, they're motivated by kindness and generosity. When one hunter or a group of them attacks a family of lions, the male doesn't hesitate to give his all to defend his family, and if he is injured or killed, the female will defend the cubs with the same fortitude and courage. Let's not delude ourselves into thinking that in similar circumstances there are differences between our human emotions and the creatures

---

1. Diallo is describing the unusual practice of allowing West African soldiers to bring their families along with them on military campaigns. The French called this *la smala*, from the Arabic word for "entourage."

we call "animals." On the contrary, it would be better to assume that every animal, like every human being, has a heart and soul endowed with intelligence and fortitude.

These women come from all the black nations of Senegal, from Upper Senegal and Niger, French Guinea and Mali, and in particular, from the Bambara, Toucouleur, Sousou, Kado, Mossi, Bobo, Kassonké, and many other peoples. They love their husbands, they follow them and they enhance the men's bravery, even in battle, and in death. Don't we realize that by their work they are serving France? They prepare meals, wash laundry, and sweetly submit to a woman's fate, but they're also strong, cheerful, and affectionate with their husbands, comforting the men who desperately need reassurance. We shouldn't dwell on their physical attributes. We should look instead into the depths of their souls. Their personal qualities and their strong sense of discipline seem to me to be more important than their appearance. The heart and the mind are all important in a person. Along with the soul, they contain the essence of humanity, God's creation.

No one tries to attack us while we're in Fez, so, except for drills and patrols around the outskirts of the camp, we live absolutely peacefully. We feel as if we're inside a casbah blessed by Peace itself. Sometimes we take walks along the river and go swimming. We wash our clothes and then go fishing while the clothes are drying under the blazing sun. We enjoy that pastime, although the fish don't appreciate it. Yesterday Amadou Ba told us he caught several little fish who were attracted by the earthworms he offered them. "It's as easy as pie. I'm teaching them how to bite." Youssouf Boubou piped up, asking him: "And why are you teaching them this?" Amadou Ba wasn't expecting that question and so he looked surprised. He grinned a little and then wiped that expression off his face, and then he grinned again, bursting out laughing. His teeth gleamed like pearls between his black lips that were stretched wide open. But all of a sudden he stopped laughing and looked around to make sure all eyes were on him. Then, he replied: "I do it to show them the sun." But while our brothers were laughing, one of us was thinking: We're cruel to pull these little fish out of the water. They die suffocating in the hot sun, strangling on the hooks that awful men have invented. Shouldn't we recognize their right to freedom, since we, too, have to live?

In the camp the infantrymen are relaxing and chatting quietly in little groups of four, five, or more. It's nine o'clock in the morning. Everything is calm. The clear blue sky is a mirror reflecting our minds' eyes. I just passed the exam for corporal cadet and since I ranked ninth out of forty candidates, I'm eligible for promotion. Sitting on the ground with my legs crossed, I'm holding a small notebook that I bought in Fez. Inside are the letters of the alphabet that a French friend of mine from the Fifth Regiment of the Colonial Infantry had written. I think: "I did well on the exam. I'm a good private first class, and despite having spent a month in the hospital during the training course for corporal cadets, I still came in ninth out of forty. I may became a corporal soon. But I barely understand French. I can neither read nor write it, and yet if I am promoted, I'll have more responsibilities. I'll get orders to carry out. I'll have to understand them perfectly. I don't want to be a soldier who makes mistakes, consciously or unconsciously, because he doesn't understand what the orders mean. I love justice, equality, and liberty. Therefore, I must learn how to speak French. It can't be that difficult. And I'll end up learning to read and understand it as well as I do my native language. I'll do it. I love it so much. I already know a few words." Then, I look at the alphabet letters: A, B, C, D, E, F . . . F . . . Oh . . . my friend has told me that to write "France," you have to put the letters in this order: F, r, a, n, c, e. Oh? That's good. Captain Coste comes toward me. He's standing right over me. Why? What's he going to say? It can't be too serious. The expression on his face is the same as always, radiating kindness. I stand up to salute him, but with a gesture, he orders me to sit back down. I'm relieved and sit cross-legged, holding my notebook in my hand. The captain is standing in front of me, not saying a word. I think: "He's not talking. He's looking at me. What could he be interested in?" I don't dare look back at him. I can't be the one to speak first. What then? "Bakary, what are you doing?" he asks in a tone of voice as kind as a doting father's. I glance at him and say, "My captain, me like read French. Me very like French." The captain picks up my notebook and reads the word "France." He leafs through the pages, again and again. He seems to looking for something on every page of the little book. His eyes narrow. He stops examining the notebook, looks at me for a long time, and pointing at me, says: "Write down here: 'La France.'" I look at the letters to find how to write "la" first of all, but I can't. I write only 'France.'[2] "That's good, Bakary. Me pleased with you. You can read France. You good boy, good soldier."[3] Then Captain Coste himself writes in my notebook "La France" and says to me: "Look here. This 'l', this 'a'; together make 'la.' Now you say 'La France.' Now you know how read French." I take back my notebook and say to the captain: "Me not know good French, my captain, not on paper, but can read French in your heart." He stands there without saying a word. I keep reading "La France" as before, gazing intently at the name that was explained to me. As he leaves, Captain Coste taps me lightly on the right

---

2. The soldiers were not taught to use articles, such as *la* or *le*, in the pidgin French used by the Colonial Army. Diallo illustrates this point with his difficulty grasping "La France" versus "France."

3. Captain Coste speaks to Diallo in *petit nègre*, the pidgin French taught in the training manual for colonial officers.

cheek and walks away as quietly as he came. Many fine things are communicated by his silence, just as I understand the mighty sun that silently illuminates the whole world.

Captain Coste is going back to France and he introduces Captain Lamothe, his replacement, to the company. He's leaving that very day! He calls us together to say goodbye. Sergeant Samba is our interpreter for Captain Coste's speech. A stunned silence prevails. I hear a few whispers among the infantrymen: "It hurts to see him leave us." Others say: "We won't have another leader like him." The soldiers are so sad, you would have thought that someone's father had died. It's all very disturbing, and Captain Coste realizes it. He's sad, too. He looks around at all the Senegalese men in his company. The soldiers who love him express it with their eyes: "Don't leave us, captain. You've become our father and we don't want to do without your presence or kindness." Standing before the company that he's led for two years with utmost, heartfelt nobility, he says: "Infantrymen, you know I'm leaving today for France, to be reunited with my family. You, too, you'll leave soon to return to your homeland, to your families. Thus, we're going to part. I'm very sorry to be leaving you. You're men, infantrymen, who are happy to serve France. That's why I care for you so much, and I'm sorry to say goodbye to the fine soldiers you've become through your own efforts. France thanks you for your loyalty. I thank you for it, too, and I'll always be glad to see you again and to command infantrymen as brave as you are." He shakes the officers' hands and then the hands of all the privates who come up to him, who gather around him, and who say to him with genuine feeling: "You good captain, good Frenchman." The captain comes over to shake my hand. He says a few words to me that Sergeant Samba translates: "To me, you've been a model serviceman." I ask Samba to tell him: "My captain, I've always considered my efforts very minor and I'm determined to sacrifice everything to demonstrate my merit and devotion to you. I'll never forget you."

We watch Captain Coste leaving the way you watch a beloved father dying. There was no difference. He had the sort of loving kindness that touches your heart and soul and makes you understand the meaning of grace. We think about it and decide that we shouldn't look for the measure of a man in his skin color, but in his mind, governed by his intelligence. That's why this very French officer was loved by us, the Senegalese, who only asked for one thing: permission to love. He gave us that. And we will always love this leader whom we've admired with our hearts and minds for two years under the harsh conditions of warfare. His kindness made us love and admire the French race which he had so nobly and impeccably represented, as we watched and learned from him in silence.

9.

Duty Calls

How we spent our time between May 1911 and July 1914—those were days to remember! We are back in Casablanca, assigned to small work details every day, supervised by the adjutant Moriba Keita, a Senegalese. Moriba knows the proverb: "Service first, comrades after." He's tall, strong, and a very competent leader. Yesterday I watched him write something in French. That really caught my attention. I also tried to imitate his fluent French pronunciation. I heard him say to a Senegalese corporal whom he had summoned: "Here is a voucher for three 'bucks'; bring it to the warrant officer in the depot." He speaks crisply and decisively, but not at all in an overbearing way.

I see a lot of my friends. Samba Diallo, Salla Diallo, and Demba are all privates first class. In the evening we often talk about our homeland. We're eager to see good old Senegal again since we left almost four years ago. The word spreads that three days from now a steamer will take us back there. We can't think about anything else, and the joyful prospect of seeing our parents again fills us with happiness. I didn't realize that getting ready for our return journey would be so sweet. We go into town to buy things, souvenirs from Morocco, the country we're leaving for Senegal . . . But suddenly, all at once, Casablanca looks and feels different. In town, a deadly silence reigns. Around the camp, inside the depots, there's a flurry of activity that I've never seen before. It's really striking. Bugles sound everywhere, calling us to muster double quick. Soldiers return to the camp and so do the firefighters. We all wonder: "What's going on?" The adjutant shouts out: "Attention!" The sergeant-major reads a dispatch out loud. It's a bit long and we only grasp two things from it: "Germany has declared war on France . . . And France calls on all her children . . ." Once we've understood, our youthful high spirits come back and we get giddier and giddier. It's incredible how a sense of excitement takes hold of us, overwhelms us, lifts our souls aloft. It overcomes so many everyday hopes and plans and makes us forget, in the blink of an eye, the immense joy we had felt at the prospect of seeing the land of our birth, our parents. We abandon those long-held desires without a second thought.

The Eighth Battalion of Senegalese Infantry leaves for France. The Seventh arrives in Casablanca from Marrakesh. All the Frenchmen eligible for repatriation are included.[1] Demba Sow leaves in the Eighth Battalion without me because I was transferred into the Seventh. I've known this great guy for four years and this is the first time we've been separated. I try to avoid our parting because I know it will be painful. I couldn't prevent it, even though I asked for a post in his battalion. I've never been so devastated, realizing that I wouldn't have Demba by my side. He is a man whose friendship, loyalty, sincerity, and wholehearted affection I've treasured. He came to say goodbye and didn't seem to have changed one bit. I could see all his distinctive personal qualities at a glance. His mind was filled with good sense, and his heart with the highest ideals of fraternity, the ones that inspired me. He didn't have any profound words to commemorate our parting but our eyes, like two bright mirrors, exchanged the brotherly feelings that our words could not express. He didn't show any outward signs of emotion, but I simply felt his goodness, the kind that even a brother may not actually have for his own blood relatives. "Bakary," he said, "farewell. On to France! And we'll try

---

1. Some French convicts and soldiers charged with disciplinary infractions were sent to serve in the African Colonial Army, so Diallo is implying that some of the French were not welcome to return.

to serve there in the same battalion." At this moment so many thoughts swarmed in my head that I was dizzy, and in response, I could only say, "Yes," and slowly nod my head. But when he is a hundred meters away, Demba stops, turns back toward me, glances at me quickly, and moves on. He turns a corner and is now behind a tent that hides him from view. Goodbye, Demba! Now indeed I know that a *labbo* is as human as a Fula shepherd and if society has established differences between them, it's simply like an army that divides us into squadrons and sections.

We're given uniforms made of thick dark material, the sleeves and collars edged with narrow yellow braid, and also shirts and sweaters. Once the uniforms are issued, the roll call begins. "So and so . . . Present . . . So and So . . . Present . . ." It lasts so long that we hear nothing else because this isn't roll call for only one section, it's for a whole battalion, a regiment, and maybe even more. With the military band leading the way, the battalion marches to the harbor where we'll board our ships. I wanted to find out if the soldiers were regretting going to France to fight rather than returning to French West Africa as we had expected. And I learned that I was the only one foolish enough to have even considered it. I felt even worse hearing my brothers in arms say the name "France" over and over so passionately, like lovers coming to the rescue of a damsel in distress while I seemed to be the only one whose thoughts strayed from France back to Senegal. My mind was filled with so many memories of home instead of sharing the men's single-minded dedication, postponing all those lovely plans with my family and concentrating on our sacred duty to answer the call of the Motherland, to say as they did: "Present."

After four days at sea, crossing the Atlantic, we land at Cette in Hérault.[2] We're glad to see a town in mainland France for the

---

2. Cette was a French town on the Mediterranean coast, near Montpellier. Since 1928, it has been named Sète.

first time. We look at the people, the houses, the streets, the tram
lines, and our eyes are caught by the sight of a huge number of
flags flying. We recognize the tricolor flag. We walk through the
town, a band leading the way, in such an impressive parade that
children, boys and girls, happily step in line behind us. You would
have thought, moreover, that the entire population of Cette had
decided to give us a fine welcome. Their shouts of "Long live
France!" and "Hooray for the Senegalese!" touch us deeply. Several
men rush out of the crowds lining the streets to shake our hands. I
hear them say "Bravo, Senegalese infantrymen! Long live France!"
Others tell us: "Cut off the Germans' heads." The soldiers smile as
they usually do and show off their *coupes-coupes* [sabers], promising
to kill all of France's enemies.

It's nighttime. The troops stroll around the town. Everyone
welcomes us and offers something to eat or drink in the cafés, the
tobacco shops, the bakeries, the butcher shops. They chat with us,
asking us where we come from. They give us money. Because of all
those welcoming gestures, we want to look more closely at their
different faces and expressions. Some are brimming with kindness;
others reveal an inner torment. We notice that occasionally their
rosy cheeks are drained of color when we talk about the war. We
understand the reason for that, and it sends shivers down our
spines. Our high spirits are going to flag. But no . . . Face-to-
face with the decency of these fine people, our spirits are like a
mast standing firm in the center of a foundering ship. Everyone
assures us that the Senegalese troops are much loved in France.
We use the few words of French we know to express the joy
and honor we're feeling. We're sorry we can't express ourselves
better. We're frustrated we can say almost nothing in reply to our
good friends in Cette, whose words touch us so much. It's easier
to communicate with the children who approach us. They're so

neat and cute that they inspire warm feelings the way a perfect angel would. A little fearful but determined, they stretch out their tiny hands to shake ours; some scrutinize theirs afterward to see if they've been blackened by our grip. That isn't surprising. It's only natural and to be expected that children would set their little brains to investigating something new. It's the only way to learn by experience.

Without seeming to, we're also watching our little friends. They must think we're children too because we're so lighthearted. Feeling more comfortable, they stretch their hands out to us again and this time they don't hesitate. They've found out what they needed to know, and we're just as pleased. I'm charmed by these childish gestures that deserve recognition by the hearts and minds of those devoted to the noble cause of fraternity. As usual, I take note of this, filing it away in my memory. I see a little girl standing in front of a butcher shop. She's probably six or seven years old, and has brown hair down to her shoulders and big, lively black eyes that look like gleaming mirrors. I enjoy the charming sight of this little French girl who's like a beacon of light shining in my eyes. Her sweet smile is a sign of her goodness, an unaffected goodness. I go up to her and say, "Little girl, much pretty." She offers me her little white hand, a gesture I appreciate, and I go back to the camp that night promising myself that I'll come and see her again.

Actually, here I am again, near her, but this time, instead of standing at the door, I go into the house to say, "Good evening." She's happy to see me and calls out, "Mama, Mama." Her mother shakes my hand, and I catch sight of her father in the dining room. Her grandmother comes up to me next, smiling, saying, "Good evening, sir." The mother asks me, good-naturedly, if I like her daughter. I say, "Yes," and she invites me to come and visit them every day before I leave for the front. What extraordinary luck.

I have a French sister! I hadn't expected to encounter whites' friendly feelings for blacks. So I often go twice in the evening to see this family. I already know the girl's name: Simone. And her father's name is Auguste Baudry. I spent a week that way. I didn't let a night go by without paying a visit to this French family. During this time, a very strong feeling dominated my thoughts. I couldn't understand how our hearts came together in such a short time, despite the powerful suspicions that usually keep human beings apart. The reason is that the power of goodness is the only tonic against prejudices. I realized that there was no need for words or the power of speech for it to be effective. It just has to be present.

Oh you people of France, you who God has chosen as our masters for so many years now, you haven't hesitated to entrust to us, like your own sons, the defense of France. You saw us work the soil of Africa with you, the land where we were born, where we were raised. You who, amid false beliefs, find justice, truth, and goodness. You are the nation that God has deemed the hope of mankind by his divine grace and by the power of your ideas, your philosophy, and your achievements. You'll see the absolute proof of our commitment to you, the proof of our loyalty and dedication that your justice will not fail to recognize after the things that will soon come to pass. Watch us very closely, as we watch you, and let us work together for the France that we both love. We'll value each other, appreciate each other, respect each other, and love each other even more. People never have enough love. From now on, before going any further, we want to thank you so much for having celebrated our arrival in your beautiful land, which we had admired so much from afar. At this time, everything in your country amazes us: the houses, the sea, the trees, the soil, the sky, your eyes, everything you do. A thousand other things charm us, too, and focus our minds on annihilating the enemy that threatens your peace of mind and your noble spirit. Fighting side by side with you, we expect to attain perhaps an even greater goal in the future, to see you justify tomorrow all the emotions we have felt witnessing the soul of the great France, a hope shared by so many of our black brothers.

Today is the day that we leave for the war, for the front and I don't want to go without saying goodbye to the Baudrys, so I get a pass and go straight to their house. I'm struggling with the thought of leaving these fine people in a few short minutes, and possibly forever. Will I be able to keep myself from crying as soon as I enter the house that has been such a sweet refuge for a week? This is a place that attracted me heart and soul, as if I were under a spell. Will I even be able to find the right words in French to express my feelings without revealing my mental anguish and heartache about leaving? In situations like this, don't tears and trembling imply the presence of fear? Besides fear, what force makes our whole body shake? Only the soul can answer these questions. I'm convinced that the joy of seeing loved ones has this effect, when we know we must leave them but don't know if we'll ever see them again. My soul is very sensitive today, like the day in Casablanca when Demba Sow left. In the handful of days and the few short hours that I've spent in Cette, my soul has been nourished by unadulterated goodness and I felt a wave of affection that I had not experienced before now. My Senegalese sisters, whom I indeed love with all my heart, had never aroused such feelings in me. Nonetheless, they loved me with all the sweetness and the generosity I could possibly have wanted. Is this because the love of friends that we encounter through God's grace is more powerful than family bonds? That's how it seems to me; I also think that my feelings for Demba Sow were more intense than my love for my brothers, and even for my father and mother. I must stress, however, that with my sisters I felt completely happy knowing that they loved me unreservedly. When I think about them and about Simone Baudry,

I have to conclude that family ties, even at their strongest, are part of human nature while accidental, deep connections with strangers raise us to totally unexpected levels of happiness. I reach my dear friends' house. First I give them a military salute, and then I shake their hands. When Madame Baudry, her mother, and Simone gather around me, I tell them our regiment has to leave for the front the next morning and that I couldn't leave Cette without thanking them for their hospitality. I read the emotion on their faces. I draw on all my reserves of military courage to keep myself calm and collected, to stay cool (like marble). Since I can't express my thoughts well in French, I can only show them my high spirits and brave attitude, and in this way, try not to distress them. Madame Baudry says to me: "You like Simone. You must write to us when you arrive. Tell us whatever you can, and we'll write back." While she is speaking, she writes their address on a blue envelope which she gives me, along with several packages of cigarettes, crackers, sardines, and other things. These gifts really touch me, not because of the things themselves, but because of the kind expression on Madame Baudry's face when she hands them to me. It's priceless. I felt as if I was receiving gifts from my own mother.

The grandmother, Madame Hugues, is standing to our left. She's lost in thought, as if she were searching among a thousand things for this bond between human beings, the essence of blessings. My keen shepherd's eye notes her distraction, the same sharp eye I had when I left the darkness of the forest to admire the light of the plains. She gazes at me with her wise eyes, imbued with goodness and the nobility of spirit that is recalling its acts of charity. Simone is leaning on her grandmother, on her right, with her tiny hand on her mother's shoulder. Her gentle eyes take in everything that is going on, but they're as sad as mine as we say goodbye. She's so cute. I feel the tears well up in my eyes, eyes that are an open window into so many of my thoughts. But I will not cry. How could a Senegalese infantryman called to duty by his homeland weep at the very moment of departure? I gather my thoughts and say goodbye to this French family whose heart has been a beacon of kindness for me.

We're facing German troops on the Marne.[3] It is four o'clock in the morning. You might say you could see the first signs of dawn. Everywhere, especially in the east, the feeble light gets stronger and the darkness recedes from the hillsides, concentrating in patches here and there, in gullies and at the foot of trees whose branches are very still. The sky grows lighter above us, like a blue eye that is opening to see something terrible happen. The rifles, cannons, and other innocent tools that kill their masters aren't making any noise. The troops are eating breakfast and drinking coffee. Everything had been prepared during the night and we need to be nourished in order to have the strength to die. A German who is mistaken about the front lines is captured. He comes in for his coffee, led by a Senegalese guard. When he is surrounded by our soldiers, he shakes from head to toe. Poor guy, didn't you ever dream about this moment when you imagined the other side of the coin—the joy and elation of victory? The black men, the ones you thought are savages, have captured you, but instead of killing you, they've made you a prisoner.[4] May your fear not prevent you from proclaiming in your homeland, tomorrow, after the battle, your allegiance to justice, a justice that will lift up all human races, all the savages. But it seems that the brief interlude of calm at first light isn't enough to make men think.

---

3. The Battle of the Marne (September 6–12, 1914) was a crucial engagement early in World War I. The French and their allies halted the German advance on Paris, near the Marne River.

4. Diallo is referring to the widespread propaganda that African soldiers beheaded their captives. The German prisoner believes he is in for savage treatment by the Senegalese troops.

The battle begins again, with the awful, sorrowful racket of cannon fire, rifles, and machine guns. A flock of pigeons rises in the air, scatters, and comes back together. I see it heading toward the branches of a tree opposite me. Keep going, poor innocent creatures; shells are knocking down your beloved roost and the whole trunk, which was standing tall to receive you in its branches, is prostrate forever. The leafy cover for your nests is inundated by the fiery breath of angry monsters. Follow the river; the Marne will guide your eyes toward Peace, toward the center of France. A few days later we're near Reims, at Sillery, in the woods. The barrage of fire is intense. Feeling the ground shaking under our feet makes us think of praying. Poor Mother Earth, the men you succored with your noble care are incapable of gratitude. They can't destroy you, so they fight each other ferociously and wound you. Thinking of your bounty that so patiently nourishes all creatures, meets all their needs, and makes men's lives as pleasant as possible, I have to ask why human beings do not grasp the unity of all life? A shell has just exploded on you, Mother Earth, then another, then six all at once, and while even more are whistling through the air to tear you apart, I can see water welling up from the holes torn in your surface. Oh, Mother Earth, why do you weep for your ungrateful sons, of whom I am the worst?

A regimental order: a corporal and the Senegalese infantry are to fight with the Randier Battalion.[5] The 1st Company of the Seventh Senegalese Battalion gets the order. The call goes out for a volunteer among the corporals. The company assembles and the officers stand facing us, papers in hand. The corporals and their men look at each other. Silence is, it seems to me, the interpreter of our unspoken words. I hear the soldiers mutter:

---

5. Lieutenant Colonel Randier commanded the 109th French Infantry. It had many battles to its credit and its men were highly decorated for bravery.

"Let's all go together." I realize at that moment that a private first class would be warmly welcomed by those crack riflemen. So . . . "Present, my captain. Me volunteer . . ." I step forward to present arms. The commanding officer comes and shakes my hand, and perhaps to encourage me, promises to reward me. That won't be necessary. Even if a soldier, like any servant, might expect special compensation, I don't feel that way in my heart or my mind. I'm only focused on the immediate future. My whole body is so hardened that I have to wonder whether God has actually changed my nature, which was so sensitive before. My entire squadron comes along with me. No one wanted to let me go alone and that thrilled me. It seems as if the German artillery knows about our plans. They fire shells at us. It's seven o'clock in the evening. The sun refuses to watch over us; the night takes over. In these thick woods, you could hardly see twenty meters ahead. Here it comes. Three shells just landed in our trench. Some men are wounded. My left arm is injured. The medics try to evacuate me with the others, but I refuse categorically. A soldier must obey, but how could I leave my squadron while I'm still alive, when they didn't want to leave me? At that moment, an officer yells: "Forward! Fix your bayonets!" With my rifle in my right hand, I press forward, ahead of my men, like a ferocious lion with fangs of iron. The Germans in the front line rain bullets on us. The incoming fusillade traces a fiery red arc, lighting up all along the lines of the trenches. The fire comes down to earth in the forest glade where dying men call out for their gods, their mothers, and their prophets, all of them far away. The ground shakes, trees topple, and men's cries mingle with the booming fire of cannons, machine guns, and rifles. The echoes, and an indefinable groaning all around us, turn these woods into a vision of hell. We press forward, but our ranks are thinning out. Half of us are wounded, and among the men who keep going, I see some die. On my right hand, one of my soldiers falls, and blood gushes from his head onto the ground as he lies there. You would have thought he had his ear pressed to the earth, listening to a faint call from its depths. I see another one stabbing a tree trunk with his bayonet. He thinks it's an enemy soldier. Sylla, who is near me, points to the man and bursts out laughing. We push forward again. We're standing on the edge of the German trench. There are only three of us left. I'm useless. I've just been wounded again, this time in the mouth. Sylla pulls me off the edge of the trench and helps me back to the French lines. At the first aid station, the doctor asks my name. There's a problem. I can't speak. My tongue has been cut in two inside my broken mouth. I could write my name instead, but my head is swollen, and my eyes see only an unnatural, swirling fog that perturbs all my senses. My ears hear next to nothing and I feel as if all the blood in my body is boiling up to them. Alongside me, I hear someone say, "He's finished . . ." but that doesn't bother me. It's as if I was indifferent to everything, even my own pain. My only thoughts are for my mother. She calls me to her and holds me tight. I feel the sweetness of that call and the sadness of the creature that she bore. At that point, my very soul is in agony, not from my wounds but because of the distance between us. Never before, since I left my family, had I summoned up that beloved image in my mind as clearly as my eyes can see the light of day.

10.

Angels Rising to Heaven

I HAD AN OPERATION AS SOON AS I ARRIVED AT THE FIELD hospital in Épernay. I was given liquid chloroform, poured on a bandage and held under the patient's nose. The patient breathes in, it circulates around the body, and the body loses consciousness, feels no pain during the operation, and wakes up afterward, astonished at this miracle. I'm still amazed by it. I wonder if I haven't had a taste of life after death. The doctor, Major Jacquemont, who was chief physician in the Trousseau clinic, is extremely kind to me. He often comes in the morning and evening, shakes my hand, asks how I'm feeling, asks if I need anything, and tells the nurses to take extra care of me. I know he doesn't treat any of the wounded men differently, so I wonder what is behind the double dose of attention that he's giving me. Is it because I'm the only African in a ward full of Europeans? Is that the reason he takes extra care of my poor self? I think so, but in any case, I wish I had been able to speak in order to say "Thank you" at the very least.

The Red Cross volunteers—Madame Thil, Mademoiselle Germaine, and Mademoiselle Louise—are kind to all the wounded men. I see Madame Thil go up to a soldier who has a head wound. His lips are opening a little because he wants to smile, but his face is twisted with pain. I realize that this gentle woman is trying to cheer up this unfortunate man. Mademoiselle Louise, a charming young woman with golden hair, is in the middle of the room, rolling a white bandage. She's going to dress the wound of the soldier facing her. The wounded man keeps his eyes on her blond hair. Keep looking, my friend; she's from an aristocratic family.

117

That thought makes me look around for Mademoiselle Germaine. I spot her next to the doctor, Major Jacquemont, who's saying something to her. No doubt he's talking about the patients. Mademoiselle Germaine smiles at me. She has noticed I'm looking at her. I feel as if she is directing endless waves of kindness to my soul, and I keep my eyes fixed on her face.

The nun who's the night monitor stands at the foot of my neighbor's bed. This man is going to die. It's about four o'clock in the morning. The darkness of the night struggles with him in the white sheets of the hospital beds, and all the comrades who are awake are watching his eyes, trapped between darkness and light. The silence of the ward is broken occasionally by a wounded man's "ooh, ooh, um, ouuuuuh." A sad sound of agony that's made even sadder by the dying man's cries of "mama . . . mama . . . my mother . . . my God . . . my God . . ." It's over. His eyes are open, staring at the ceiling as if they still saw something there. The other wounded men look at each other, without saying a word. They realize that the man who had just died was someone just like them. The nun dressed in her habit is standing, hands clasped in front, head high, eyes wide open, lips moving. She's absorbed in prayer, and the sight of her overwhelms my heart. I'm a poor sensitive man who has forgotten who and where he is. I watch the rays of sunlight creep into the room through the window panes. The sister prays, still standing motionless. I get the feeling she's no longer the same person; she has become someone else, ready to soar into heaven like an angel.

11.

Gris-Gris

I LEFT ÉPERNAY A FEW DAYS AGO. I WAS ADMITTED TO THE FIELD hospital in Neuilly-sur-Seine. My wounds aren't healing and I feel as if they're more painful since I left Épernay. I have terrible dreams at night: I burrow into the earth, searing my head in a horrendous fire that engulfs me; the heat forces me out, but I leap out of the fire only to go back in again. Sometimes I am so upset that I wake up covered in sweat. I don't know what causes these nightmares. The frequency of these torments puts me on edge and disturbs me even when I'm awake. At night when it's time to sleep, I resist falling asleep with every fiber of my being, and my eyes refuse to close. It's only during the day that I'm able to sleep, but just a little. Obviously, all of this discourages me. I take the precaution of forcing my mind to summon up the opposite of the feelings I have from time to time. I remember what Thierno Alassane told me in Ndar before I left Senegal: "Whenever you're in trouble, concentrate on your *gris-gris* and the difficulty will disappear before your very eyes." So I vow to concentrate on my *gris-gris* that night before I try to sleep . . .

Something strange has just happened. Around six o'clock in the evening, as I was thinking about my amulets, a nurse brings me a little package that was wrapped with care and addressed to me: "Corporal Bakary Diallo." I open it. Inside are my amulets, what we call *gris-gris*, the protective talismans I had left behind at Épernay. The kind lady volunteers had forwarded them to me and ever since I got them back, I was able to sleep peacefully, freed from the awful nightmares that had tormented me. Are *gris-gris* more powerful than bullets in these circumstances?[1]

I was astonished by this bizarre coincidence for quite a while. But, alas, *gris-gris*, though they provide striking proof of the power of the human imagination, are really nothing more than some rare herbs, tender sprigs of plants growing in the wild, valuable roots or vines cut off the trees they climb. They are made from preserved boars' hearts (the boars that menaced our villages), bits of straw that hadn't burned in our bonfires, monkeys' tails sliced off by the traps set by hunters and shepherds, snakes' heads, dead men's teeth, rat hair, and elephant hair. The ingredients would be put in an animal horn, or wrapped in a piece of cloth or in a rabbit hide or goatskin. You poor inert materials, I say, that living beings believe to be holy, with a faith born from centuries of belief, what mysterious powers do you have? What powers do men attribute to you, in secret or in public? How do we explain why humans, who are so afraid of death and even of pain, invented you to believe in you when they go to war? And I, an insignificant member of the human race, why can't I understand that the strongest charms are the rules of love? Instead, I spend my time on earth thinking about you, destroying you, pillaging you, in order to make my talismans and adorn myself with them. What sort of creature am I?

---

1. Many soldiers of the Great War carried good luck charms with them. Paul Fussell documented British soldiers' fondness for such charms in *The Great War and Modern Memory* (New York: Oxford University Press, 1975), 124.

12.
In Paris

AFTER A BRIEF STAY IN NEUILLY, I WAS SENT TO THE Lariboisière Hospital in Paris, near the Gare du Nord. I'm under the care of Professor Sébilleau, a surgeon and the head of the Isambert wing, which is filled with wounded soldiers from all of France's armies. Days and nights go by, almost without my noticing them, so blinding is the whiteness of the rows of hospital beds that are lined up under the electric lights blazing in these sparkling clean rooms. It's a cloudless sky designed and built by men to shelter the patients escaping from hell, who come there to heal the damage inflicted by the flames. This inferno was ignited by the gods, who are astounded by the fire they set off. Sundays are the only days that stand out. This is when visitors, relatives, friends, or even strangers who want to help the wounded soldiers come.

Madame Wilfort, a distinguished relative of Dr. Sébilleau, seems to want to extend her generosity to each and every wounded man.[1] She comes almost every morning, bringing café au lait, chocolate, tobacco, and cigarettes for us patients, cheering up the sad soldiers. When she found out I had had an operation the day before, she came to my bedside. I had swallowed my tongue during the operation and in order to save my life, Dr. Sébilleau had been called in to cut open my neck and insert a breathing

---

1. Madame Wilfort is one of many French women Diallo encountered during his recovery who were known as *marraines de guerre* (wartime godmothers). The government encouraged these women to look after the welfare of African soldiers by visiting them in hospital, writing letters for them, and giving them gifts of food and tobacco.

tube. As a result, I was in terrible pain and had a lot of trouble breathing. I felt very weak, lying flat on my bed and thinking I might die at any moment. So many thoughts rush into my mind. I'm so anxious that I feel as if my bones are shivering with cold and then shaking with heat. As one thought slips away, others vibrate in my head, and I have a vision of a circle of light. Inside it is my dear mother, reaching for me. I see scenes of my childhood, like in a film. I revisit the villages I loved, the fields I ran across, the rivers I swam in, the trees I climbed, my boyhood friends, my dear sisters, my brothers, my father—my whole life in Senegal unfolds before my eyes. My eyes, which had been closed, open gradually, and I see Madame Wilfort, kind and dignified, watching the changing expressions on my face with profound sadness. I make a gesture to her, asking for a sheet of paper to write on, and she hands it to me. I write: "My mother, me going to die, I greet you, my mother . . ." Madame Wilfort leaned over to find out what I wanted to say in those very badly written lines scrawled by my weak hand. An expression of terrible sorrow flashed across her face. When I saw that, I seemed to forget my own suffering. I was dumbstruck, shocked, unable to control my thoughts. I gazed into Madame Wilfort's eyes as if I saw my own mother, Diara, in her even though she and my mother were different colors. Can the soul of a woman who takes the place of an absent mother become one and the same with her? Madame Wilfort exclaimed, "Don't cry any more, Diallo, or I won't come to see you again." And the idea that she wouldn't come to see me any more transformed me. I felt a sense of calm that eased my pain a little. My benefactress understood that, and she kept on showering me with kindness.

Professor Sébilleau had me moved to another hospital at 49, rue La Boétie, where he was an attending physician. I was sorry to leave Lariboisière Hospital where I appreciated the excellent treatment by the staff in the Isambert wing. I also missed the wonderful volunteers who came on Sundays to visit the patients. I was depressed, thinking that Mademoiselle Germaine Thoury and her friend wouldn't come to see me any more. Her visits had cheered me up. As Sunday approached, I'd be tormented by a vague feeling of impatience. There she was in my mind's eye: tall, brunette, her black eyes brimming with kindness, with a beautiful smile that made her even more charming and attractive. When she arrived, between two and three in the afternoon, I could pick out her footsteps from those of all the other visitors filling the ward. Her confident stride would slow down as if she were taking care not to disturb my rest, or if she thought I was sleeping, she tiptoed in so as not to wake me. Ah! If only she knew how eagerly I waited for her lovely presence. As soon as she reached my side, I could ignore for a moment the devilish torment of my wounds. Gazing at her kind eyes and her gleaming, clean hair, hearing her ask me how I was doing, I felt as if I was actually seeing one of the girls in the heavenly paradise that the Fula in Senegal call "*Ourolaïmi*."[2]

And just as the sky shelters the entire earth, the goodness of the French was obvious everywhere. A few days later, when I was going to see Dr. Sébilleau, I was sitting in a tram across from a dark-haired man with bright, optimistic eyes. He glanced at me from time to time, taking a closer look. His gaze swept over my head, wrapped in a bandage, and the military medal pinned to my chest. Since there was nothing surprising about someone looking at a wounded soldier, I didn't bother wondering what else might have sparked his interest. But when I got up to leave the tram with my friend Richard, he got up, too, and with his hat in his hand, he asked my name and address. I answered him immediately, thinking he must be a superior officer out of uniform because he

2. *Ourolaïmi* (heavenly maidens) from the Arabic *hoor al-ayn*. In Islamic belief, these angelic creatures accompany the faithful in paradise.

had a blue ribbon on his lapel, a rosette that resembled the one officers wore. Still, I tried to figure out what motivated the actions of this officer who was so polite and kind and I found out soon enough. He came to the hospital the next morning, bringing a box with a military medal inside and a business card on which he had written: "To the brave Senegalese infantryman Diallo. Young man, Chance caused me to notice you in the tram. Your wound, and the green and yellow ribbon you were undoubtedly awarded for it, caught my eye. Please allow me to give you this little memento as a token of my admiration and my respect for one of France's courageous defenders." It was signed "Henri Corlieu, Professor at the École des Hautes Études Commerciales, Paris, March 3, 1915." I wrote back to Professor Corlieu and told him that if I was one of the brave men that fought for France, he was undoubtedly one of the professors that taught men about human decency and French goodness. The courage, fortitude, and unshakable faith that sustain all the children of the homeland—don't they spring from the country's system of education? I believe I can see a new enlightenment in which reason, strength, and justice are taking shape, as clearly as you see a flock of white sheep leaving a dark wood. I'm their shepherd. I'm convinced that if human beings would only use respect and admiration in their dealings with one another, and based their judgment on facts alone, there would be no more war, which buries us alive in an abyss of suffering.

I left the hospital on rue La Boétie as I had the one on rue Lhomond, near the Pantheon; now I'm at the Rollin Hospital on avenue Trudaine. But my benefactors haven't abandoned me, as often happens when someone leaves. I'm still so pleased, especially on Thursdays and Sundays, when among the huge crowd of visitors, I see coming toward me, smiling with goodness and overflowing with mercy, a fair number of the kind French people whom I have known for several months now. Among them I cannot fail to mention Mademoiselle Albertine Velty, as well as her sister and friends. Since they would come every visiting day at exactly 2:15, I got into the habit of being ready for their arrival at that time, which they did with military precision. As soon as they arrive, they give me a kiss, one by one, starting with Albertine, and then lead me out to a bench in the courtyard, since they think I look tired. I enjoy looking at their lovely heads, their clean hair, their cheeks shining with youth and beauty, but my glance always lingers most on their smiles, because I feel as if I'm seeing once again the smiles of my own sisters gathered around me. I feel so much friendship for these fresh and charming young women. Their irrepressible liveliness whenever they visit me at Rollin Hospital dispels the silence that weighs down a lonely heart. They leave me as soon as they see the Corlieu family arrive, or some other benefactor, such as the Jullian family. If I ask them to stay with me, along with these other fine people, Albertine always finds an excuse: "It's impossible." And despite all my pleading, I let them go. They leave, reaching out their hands to say goodbye, hands that I shake very warmly.

It was only later, when Albertine came alone one day, that I understood why they left as soon as the other visitors arrived. I thought of this girl as my own sister, so I wasn't afraid to speak to her frankly. "Little Albertine, me don't know why Jeanne and friends leave when my other friends come?" Albertine was trapped. She didn't expect these questions; her cheeks flushed and her lips moved as if to speak before she closed them tight. Her smile vanished, her big eyes narrowed, and her forehead creased in a tiny frown. But as she saw me watching her, a new wave of courage smoothed away the distress that I had caused her and that I was beginning to regret. Albertine felt, as I did, caught between reluctance and decisiveness: whether to explain her reasons or refuse to answer these indiscreet questions. I thought she would find a way to avoid speaking as frankly as a sister would, so I took hold of her hand, at the pulse point that doctors use to test for a fever, and said: "Little Albertine, I hurt you, I know. Forgive me."

"Oh, why do you say 'Sorry'? You've the right, Diallo, to ask me about anything that bothers you or interests you, to ask me anything about me or whatever else, since we're more like brother and sister than just friends." "Ah." "If it wasn't you, I would keep it to myself and not tell you why we leave before the end of visiting hours, though we'd rather stay. But I can't hide from you these things that you want to understand. This is it: the other people visiting you belong to a much higher class, both in education and in wealth. They see things differently than we do, and if we stayed with you then, we might say some things that they might misunderstand or that might upset them. You can see this better if you think about the differences between their clothes and ours, I mean, me and my friends." Albertine glanced down at her dress, which was made of a simple fabric but had the virtue of cleanliness. I paid very close attention to her frank answer. I looked directly at her, surveying her from head to toe. My heart wanted to speak and my mind probed into the depths of my memory to translate my Senegalese thoughts into French. But my effort was like the hook on a fishing line bobbing to and fro like a living thing in the current of a stream; my words were like the fish that refused to take the bait. My hand trembled a little as I took hold of hers. A wave of tender feelings made me grip my friend's hand tightly.

Albertine was looking closely at me. Her eyes shone with a new brightness, perhaps a sign of her innate nobility coming to my rescue. "Little Albertine, Africa also has men, women, and everything else, but sometimes not the same clothes or the same beliefs. Still, they're men or women, nothing more. African robes or European suits, not the same words or the same customs, but all are good, useful, and just as worthwhile. Not everyone is rich, just as not everyone is poor. The best man or woman has what the French call 'goodness,' and the Senegalese call '*molsdiéré.*'

"You're very kind, because you have a big heart. I know it. You come from far away, near the Pantheon. You travel a long way to visit the wounded men, the patients who are really suffering. You're not rich but you bring cigarettes, candies, and most of all, your smile. All of that, little Albertine, is goodness. No one can do better. The other visitors who come to the hospital can't do any more than that, whether they're rich or poor. Sometimes a child who makes a small 'o' is as good as the adult who makes a capital 'O.'" (I made a circle with my index finger to explain this point.) "Rich people understand this very well. '*Molsdiéré*' is the utmost for a man or a woman.[3] Next Sunday, you'll stay with me and everyone else till the end of visiting hours. The Corlieu family and the Jullian family are my friends. They're also good people. I've told them about you. They'll be glad to speak with you, as they are with me." I had the impression that the more I talked, the more easily the French words came to my mind. I saw that the look on Albertine's face changed from a frown to the gentle expression that is natural to her, and this made me feel more at ease. I spoke softly, unconsciously lowering or raising the tone of my voice, depending on the point I was making. Now she broke out in a big smile. Her lips were more graceful than ever, and they charmingly revealed two rows of gleaming white teeth.

"So?"

"I've got it, Diallo."

"No more leaving before the visiting hours are over?"

"I'll stay till the end, since that's what you want."

---

3. The title of Diallo's memoir, *Force-Bonté*, might be his attempt at translating into French the Fula concept of *molsdiéré*, the utmost good that each person can render.

"And your sister Jeanne and your little friends too, right?"

"I'll ask them to. It will be more fun that way."

"Ah . . . , ah . . . , so kind, so kind. Thank you very much."

At that moment, truly, happiness wrapped us in its gold and silver mantle.

13.

Menton

I THOUGHT I WAS DREAMING WHEN I SPOTTED AN ARMY BASE and soldiers in red fezzes,[1] one kilometer past the train station in Menton, to the left of the tracks. No doubt, the speed of the train, the fatigue of the journey, the sleepiness that made my eyes close, and the thoughts racing around my brain had produced that effect. An idea took shape in my mind, but then it disappeared. Perhaps it was blown away by the shrieking of the locomotive's whistle. I wondered whether a miracle had transported me to a place where Senegalese soldiers, whom I hadn't seen for months and months, lived.[2] As soon as I got to the camp, these guys, so fierce in battle, were crowding in from all sides to greet me, smiling, grabbing hold of my hands, saying "*Diam Niali*" ("Hello" in Fula), "*Eni Segué*" ("Hello" in Bambara), "*Diam kam*" ("Hello" in Wolof), et cetera, as if we had known each other for a long time, even though I only recognized one man among them. This was Samba Diallo, my Fula comrade, who had been with me when I first joined up in 1911. I looked around for Demba Sow. I would have been glad to see him, even wounded, like all the convalescents, but he wasn't there. Where was he? Samba Diallo didn't know. He said simply, "*Mi alssi o fidahka deih oumimi to Sillery*," meaning, "When I left Sillery, he was there and not injured." That was in the Marne. We kept asking the newly arrived wounded men about him.

---

1. The red fez was a distinctive part of the uniform of the *Tirailleurs Sénégalais*.

2. Menton was one of several winter camps for African soldiers in the south of France. See Introduction, pp. 16–17.

Thursdays and Sundays are the days we go off base into the town. As those days get closer, the base gets livelier. All the infantrymen get ready for it, except the most seriously wounded and the sickest who don't want to or can't leave. So, this is the time for the men to get haircuts, either Senegalese style or French style, to wash our shirts, tunics, handkerchiefs, and caps. We use *tiorides* (a little piece of wood with a handle) to make our teeth even more brilliantly white. We take particular care of our nails too and trim them carefully. Some of the men, who prefer African standards of beauty, sometimes put *n'gueldi farro* on their nails to tint them red.[3] This strange expression means "the color of pride." When you wash your hands, the red gradually begins to fade, and after a short time, there's only a trace left that disappears like all too-obvious attractions. A discerning eye can categorize the men according to their tastes. Some were smitten with European sophistication; others upheld their local traditions. I decided to discuss this with Haby, a man who was cleaning his teeth at that moment and about to put on his town clothes. "Haby, why don't you buy a toothbrush to use on your teeth, since they are naturally white?" Haby gazed at me calmly and turned away so as not to break out in a smile. He seemed hesitant to answer me, or he was searching for an answer. But as I was going to add something, he hurriedly began to speak: "Corporal Bakary, *voni gonga ko ni: an-e vovi kabaroudji di leïdi; mi, Kabaroudji Sénégal Tane gandoumi*," meaning: "Corporal Bakary, here's the truth. You're accustomed to things in this land. Me, I only know about things from Senegal." I agreed with him, laughing and taking care that our conversation was open and fraternal. A few minutes went by as I struggled with the dilemma of how to ask my friend Haby more questions now that he's all ready to leave for town. Not far away I heard the sound

---

3. Diallo is describing the use of henna, a plant dye, to tint fingernails red.

of a melancholy-sounding song performed by a Fula. This song was popular in Sangom, the big town used as winter quarters, in the Dierry south of Podor (the land that was farmed only in winter).

> *Diamma dievé deih baïli*
> *Doutt'e m'berdé to djimdi belli*
> *Arr ah m'Bourré dieen*
> *E m'Bedda Sangom, Dieveten* . . .
> The night is deeper when the *baïli* (a musical instrument)
> Enters hearts where songs are sweet
> Come, oh M'Bourre, we'll go
> To the Avenue of Sangom, we'll chat.

The singer made me think of another question to ask Haby, who was also listening to the song. "So you are almost on your way to town. Are you going there to pick out a beauty among the young flowers of the Alpes-Maritimes?" "If one of them happens to find me along the way and allows me to say hello to her." "Then perhaps this is the reason your teeth are even shinier than usual?" "Could be. But just as flowers shrink from the heat, the young ladies of Menton avoid black men.[4] If only they smiled and had the courage to find out that in my heart, there's nothing but pure affection for them." Haby stopped there and gave me a crisp salute. I didn't have time to reply or even to return the salute. He was on his way.

Tierno Amadou, sitting on the ground, legs crossed, prayer beads in his hand, and his face turned to the east, is making his afternoon prayers. About thirty soldiers gather around him, and one by one, more arrive and join the group. They pray to Allah for a victory for the beloved French Army, they pray for a quick end to the war and they ask to return soon to their families in Africa.

---

4. There were attempts, not always successful, by the French authorities to limit the interaction between African soldiers and white women. See Introduction, p. 18.

The sky is blue, the sun is shining, the breeze is blowing, and the mountains are visible northeast and northwest of the coast. In the village a bell is ringing. You might think the echo comes from the smoke rising from the chimneys on the roofs in Menton, while big waves are crashing against the shore, sending up plumes of white foam that remind me of sheep being chased by wolves. Near the base I see a young woman carrying a bunch of flowers, walking toward the Borigo valley. Tierno Amadou, your black prayer beads are slipping smoothly through the first two fingers of your right hand. Are they moving like the eternal wheel of life? If not, what are you counting off that way? Is it the number of days that have gone by, or the number of days ahead for this tragedy? Will I be able to decipher their meaning and intention though they do not answer me? The dance of moral mysteries. And you, immense sky above, who cries in winter and becomes punishing in summer, will enlightenment for humankind come from you, to whom all eyes turn? And you, moon, gentle light, that wakes up the world at night and reveals true beauty, and you, the stars, the mysterious signs of the firmament where angels worship? Aren't all of these the basis of science, of virtue, of grace, and of truth? And you, air, that stirs ceaselessly around this astonishing creation that is the earth, is there any element that is more necessary? Oh, Mother Nature, countless beings live in you. Your movements and your sounds are languages that science will interpret correctly one day. Allow me to believe you have earned the name of mother, for the sake of maternal love. You shelter so many things . . . Ring, ring, keep ringing until you have attained your goal, dear bell. Ring out for universal peace for all mankind.

Sweet lovelies, fragile kindness, morning joy, flowers, you bloom by opening up into smiles that mean so much. May your scent guide my dreams. May your little buds blossom into ever more beautiful colors. No one denies your importance on earth.

The most seductive girls gaze at you. Their hearts are entranced by your power, and they love you. In order to capture women's affection, men see you as sure signs of grace and youth. They, too, are stunned by your beauty, and mistake you for gold or the colors of dawn. Your life is short, but during that time, you are celebrated with more praise and love than even the most celebrated Sprite with magic powers.

I just got out of prison on the base after serving four days. I was sentenced to eight, but the captain in charge of the convalescent center arranged to have it reduced to four. The reason I was put in jail was that I had protested, asking for a special diet: milk, mashed potatoes, and occasionally, for a little variety, ground beef or eggs. My mouth had been injured on the battlefield and I couldn't chew my food. This affected me in a way that shouldn't be ignored. My stomach certainly felt it. My health too. Major G certainly knew it. He had examined me two days after I arrived at the base in Menton. Nevertheless, he punished me when I came to tell him: "Head Doctor, Sir, I can't chew very well. I would like a special diet (*régime spécial*)." "Get lost, won't you? Just a minute, I'm going to f...ing give you eight days in lock-up. You'll get it . . . the regimental special (*régime spécial*)!"[5] I was looking at him, and as he spoke, in a rage, his eyes and his face became redder and redder. He grabbed the poor table in front of him with both hands, as if he wanted to smash it. He ordered the two Senegalese nurses who were there to take hold of me and f...ing chuck me out. But these soldiers knew me and didn't dare follow that order. In addition, they felt sorry for me. For me, the strangest part was that instead of getting angry, I stayed calm and observed the effects of the emotions overwhelming him. Anger has an amazing power.

---

5. The pun in French on the phrase *régime spécial* (meaning "special diet" and "special treatment") does not translate very well into English.

It takes a man, shakes him, agitates him to such a degree, and then leaves him ashamed of losing control. In this way, it can easily overpower even an educated man who knows full well its causes and consequences. What actually are we men like, deep inside? Why did he sentence me to prison for having requested, in the convalescent ward, the kind of nourishment that would keep me alive? I really couldn't understand it. In any case, I didn't think it was deliberate. Sometimes we all do things that our consciences couldn't imagine.

Let's forget that and watch the sea in motion. It caresses Menton with gentle waves. We can hear that deep rumble from here. The waves pick up pebbles and drop them on the smooth sand, the sound echoing like a quiet prayer. The houses in town have their windows wide open to let in the pure air. Together, let's admire the infinite number of rose-colored rays of sunlight that we see at the edge of the watery expanse that separates us from another land. Small groups of soldiers quietly gather on the seashore in the blazing sunshine between the Carlton Hotel and the Prince of Wales Hotel, which are both being used as temporary hospitals. Toward the west a group of Bambaras are playing drums. These black performers are doing the dances of Mali and they make a circle around a comic dancer, clapping their hands wildly. He flails his feet, head, and arms so that you might think there's an electric current in his body, flowing in response to the joyful crowd. You can see his left arm flung out in front, then reeled back in slowly to the side or in front, or arched over the top of his head to grasp his right hand, that was turning, turning as if it wanted to grasp the air, rotating in circles, with the audience's eyes eagerly tracking each movement. Meanwhile, his feet stamp on the ground, touching down here and there under the superb control of the dancer. This catches the attention of passers-by, of more and more Europeans who come to watch. Over the noises from the town and the sounds of the Menton surf, over the rhythm of the drums, we hear the happy song:

Badialla Mané eh . . .

Badialla Ma Tieni ô . . .

Proun, proun, ticki poum, poum, proum, proum . . .

Locals out for a stroll are walking between the drummers. Some come from the center of town and others from the vicinity of Roquebrune-Cap-Martin. They stop in front of each group of soldiers—Fulas, Wolofs, Bambaras, Susus, et cetera—and look at these carefree devils, who are forgetting their wounds for a moment, their pains, and their worries about the war, who abandon themselves, body and soul, to their African ways. And then the waves join in. First they move in a way that resembles the "bear dance," retreating slowly toward the depths of the sea, then hurling themselves up on the dry land, sending up a powerful spray. The sun watches over their movements and aims its silvery rays as if it's pitted against the moisture, except for *Dandé Mayo* (the seashore in Fula). Two trams filled with day-trippers are headed toward the western hills, about forty meters away. If we didn't know we were looking at men and women, we would have thought they were elephants running toward the savanna of Roquebrune-Cap-Martin.

Now, dozens of colored umbrellas catch the eye. They appear suddenly, everywhere, like the stars in the sky that never fall to earth. With all these things to tempt our gaze here, the sight of the parasols adds a lovely touch, a hypnotic effect when they dip from left to right, or from right to left. The strollers are dodging the surf spray in that way, and occasionally, they show their faces underneath the umbrellas, smiling or sad. Ah . . . When you're alone and you focus your eyes and your mind on the whole lively scene, the crisscrossing movement of these people and these

things, of the sky and the sea, of the trees and the air, you have
to open your soul to profound thoughts, contemplating nature's
bounty with all of your bodily senses. Look sharp! Dr. Maclaud
walks by the drummers with his family. All the soldiers stand
up straight and check that their fezzes are on straight, too. But
instead of telling the drummers to stop, the *griot* ends his frenetic
vocalizing. He leaves the center of the circle and silently creeps in a
mischievous way in front of the head doctor of Menton's hospitals,
who is in uniform decorated with four gold stripes. The wounded
men assemble here and there, and they salute the man they call
the "infantrymen's father." The doctor, who is a bit surprised by
this unexpected welcome amid a crowd of onlookers, keeps on
walking toward Hospital 252 as he acknowledges and returns the
salutes with his right hand, passing from group to group, from
soldier to soldier. His face radiates the paternal kindness that has
earned him the title of "papa," the finest and worthiest name for
all men.

   The evening shadows slowly stretch down the mountainsides
and reach the shore. Toward the east, the sea is covered with a black
mantle. The sun, a round red ball low on the horizon, sends its
golden rays over the approaching shadows. I don't know whether
this is a sign of its incomparable victory or a measure of its mercy,
since it hesitates to envelop in shadow the entire earth that it had
just illuminated. Or is this just an optical illusion that reminds
us of emotional farewells? Now the strollers on the seaside head
back to the town's streets and houses, in trams or cars, on bicycles
or on foot. The black soldiers, the convalescents, start moving,
but not to go back to the hospital right away. Instead, they make
sweeping gestures, turning their heads and hands from west to
east, fixing their eyes on the hypnotic allure of living nature. The
men and women out for a stroll go back home as quickly as they
can. Companionship, the joy of families seated around tables

set with steaming dinner plates, teasing mixed in with smiles, laughs, and childish jokes that disappear into the language of kisses, caresses, and compliments, all this is waiting for them in the brightly lit household of love. Oh, Senegalese soldiers, your color does not fear the darkness of the night. Stay a while longer, look at everything, listen to the sounds of the sea. The kind words whispered by the waves will soothe your heart with the rhythms of memories that are rooted like perennial plants deep inside you. Listen carefully. Try to hear the voices of your loved ones speaking to you from far away.

I happen to see Abdoul, his eyes tender and expressive, gazing at a group of young women walking to the center of Menton. I want to tease him because he is a tough guy but also like the "rabbit who kissed a flower."[6] "Good Lord, Abdoul, I believe you're staring." Abdoul ignores my words and keeps looking. He makes a small, involuntary motion with his head, forward and then back that makes me realize he's keeping his emotions in check. I persist. "Abdoul, from that slight movement of your head . . . I'm guessing . . ." He says nothing. I remind myself that Senegalese men, who are in general very reserved, appreciate neither indiscretion nor curtness. And I immediately regret how I've treated this good fellow. I shut my mouth.

I notice that Libettaké, the infantryman, is standing next to us. He's one of the best *griots*, and doesn't know and never has known either the silence of discretion or the reserve that comes from shyness. Libettaké is a lively man, warm, with a ready wit. He enjoys joining in the most raucous conversations. He doesn't need an invitation. He invites himself into all sorts of Senegalese business. With his mischievous spirit, like that of a monkey, he's

---

6. The phrase, "rabbit who kissed a flower," refers to a children's song: *Pan, pan petit lapin des champs*, about a wild rabbit who is "a joker, but not naughty . . . never chomped on a flower, but kissed it instead."

been observing Abdoul and his preoccupation with the young ladies of Menton, and he's also watching me. When he sees me move away so as not to keep annoying our friend Abdoul, he jumps in: "Hey . . . Ha, ha, ha, ha . . . Hey, you . . . you two there, Bakary and Abdoul, one admiring a handful of stars and the other admiring the whole picture. Ha, ha, ha, ha . . . Really you're both too funny! So why, Abdoul, don't you admit to us what your burst of admiration is about? Is there anything surprising or unusual about it? Don't you have a right to sniff the intoxicating perfume of these young blooms of Menton? When they walked by us, I saw, as Bakary did, how your eyes aimed at the one on the left who has an adorable smile. Korka, who is an expert in such matters, called her a miracle . . . He'd admit it right away." Then Korka says, "I'm always ready to discuss questions of beauty. As for that lovely we were just observing, I'll tell you what I think. I have to say, however, right away that I'm afraid I can't express nearly as well the powerful emotions that you let fly before me. Libettaké, so lighthearted, so alert, has a clever mind, a good memory, and something else, too, that's hard to put a finger on. But in short, the word 'miracle' that I blurted out instinctively when this most attractive young lady walked by is the only word that sums up adequately how I feel . . ." Libettaké continues, "*Doum ko gonga labbdo.*" ("This is the naked truth.") "And then for . . ." Ba interrupts, "Excuse me, Libettaké. Let Korka continue." Korka says, "Not at all, my dear Ba, I've said my piece. Let's have Libettaké, a fantastic *griot* with words, do the job of telling the story. He always unearths, in the depths of things, the *tobes* (points) that I would have a hard time finding even out in the open, on the sand." Libettaké responds, "It's as easy as swallowing a warm mouthful of couscous. Abdoul was captivated by this girl's looks and his enchantment overwhelmed us, too. We're dazzled, having gone into all the details of this seduction with which our love-struck friend Abdoul's heart is, perhaps, struggling." Finally

Abdoul answers: "Only God knows exactly how idiotic you are, all of you, if you haven't got anything better to do than to mock, to tease me with the excuse that I was looking at that charming girl, whom you can hardly see in the distance. Oh well, yes, I was gazing at the Italian girl, whose eyes burn like coals. I was admiring the sight of her white teeth between her smiling lips. They look like white foam on top of fresh milk. I watched her until she turned at the house across the street. If she hadn't disappeared from sight, I would have kept admiring her beauty. But my regret is still pursuing her. It is following her footsteps, guided somehow, I don't know how." Libettaké says, "A subtle perfume marks the lovers' pathway and the most determined one who breathes it in can sniff out the prettiest."Abdoul looks closely at us, the way a wolf flushed out by a hunter looks to see if there is only one enemy nearby. Ba, who has been taking it all in quietly, hurries to seize his chance to say a word or two. "Abdoulaye, we're not hunting. We're still only simple soldiers.""Who don't shoot at wolves," says Korba. We burst out laughing, clapping our hands and looking at each other in turn. Abdoul does the same.

Another soldier, Ibrahim, whispers, "*Mackou!* (Silence!) If the Europeans see us, they'll call us 'naughty boys.'" Sidibé, a Bambara, who speaks Fula and understands it even in his sleep, is listening to our chatter. He takes advantage of the time we're laughing like crazy men to call out in his native language: "Hey you over there, you Fula slaves, you aren't convalescents any more. Go play in the fight against the Germans!" Libettaké responds, "Sidibé and Sangaré, don't get upset. We'll still have a chance to laugh in the face of the ones you've mentioned." Yet, the irrepressible Libettaké feels we're straying too far from our original topic. He tries again to capture in words the charms of the Italian girl. "Which one among us," he says, "wants more than to talk a bit about the lady whose perfume is leading us . . . ah . . . where? I don't know where. Ah! Regret." Abdoul, who isn't dumb, gives us a challenge: "This hilarious Libettaké is truly invincible. Because it's so much fun, I suggest that each of us tells a story that we'll analyze together afterward." Libettaké laughs, "About the best Menton girl, no doubt. Ha, ha, ha, ha." Korka says, "No, don't laugh, guys. Let's talk seriously." "Okay, let's get started," says Libettaké. Abdoul asks, "May I begin, since I suggested it?" "Tell us, tell us, Abdoulaye," cries Libettaké. Abdoul suggests, "Bakary, you can write our stories down on paper, so nothing is missing, right?" Libettaké says, "Don't worry about them being forgotten. We all have, and you especially, a head like a fountain pen, a mind like an inkwell, a memory like ink, and a brain like paper."

So Abdoul begins: "It was evening. The animals left their burrows and other hiding places that they used as refuges in the bush during the day to look for food. All of a sudden, a rat came across a big pile of beans. The rat wanted to carry them off, but a rabbit that was bigger than the rat wanted to beat him and take them by force. When the rat realized this, it cried out loudly, 'Elephant!' Afraid of being trampled by the elephant, the rabbit raced into the shelter of the forest. And the rat carried the beans one by one into its lair, singing as it went. That's the end of my story. You're next, Korkadijo."

Korka is a bit of a comedian. He rolls up the sleeves of his military tunic, taps his head, opens his black eyes wide, curls his tongue over his lower lip, and then begins: "The hospital I was in before I came here was in a small town, whose name I don't know. I don't know the right way to dig a hole in my box to store away the names of things." When he says this, he taps his head with one finger. "Nuns ran the hospital. They were very good with the wounded soldiers. They loved God-Allah so much that they asked everyone who could walk to go to the church-mosque on Sunday to attend mass. I decided to attend with a group of patients who were going to pray to please the sisters and God. Unfortunately, I didn't know then, and still don't know now, how to pray in the Catholic manner. I wanted to pray anyway. I joined in the hymn because they were singing '*Mani ya.*' They were playing music to accompany us. In the middle of the hymn, when I was singing out in a loud voice, someone in front quickly turned around to look at me. Trying to figure out why he was looking at me, I thought perhaps I wasn't singing well or not loud enough. I wanted everyone there to hear me. I sang, softly with everyone, and then I raised my voice high enough to reach up to the church ceiling when the others lowered theirs. I sang: '*Mani ya . . . oh . . . Mani ya . . . ah . . Mani ya.*' I thought I had done just right, when to my surprise a man came to ask me to leave![7] A few minutes later, in the dining hall at lunch, the other wounded men teased me. They weren't singing then, but me, I wasn't laughing."

While we laughed uproariously, Ba mulled over what he was going to say. He scratched the back of his neck with his left hand and brought it, fingers spread apart, up to the top of his head. He wasn't trying to catch a flea. This was the way, he explained, that he grasped his thoughts. "A short time before I was called up for military service, I really enjoyed lying under a certain tree, waiting for the arrival of a certain turtledove, my sweetheart. We spent so many evenings under that tree, enjoying the perfect harmony and understanding of two hearts that love each other, but for a long time I wasn't able to speak of love to Paullèle. Often I tried to talk about the nice things that I imagined in my mind, but some kind of sorcerer hobbled my tongue and made me say the same phrase again and again: 'Ah . . . , you see, Paullèle, the moon and the moonlight . . .'"

---

7. Korka mixed up "Maria" with "*Mani-ya*," which means, in Fula, "someone is leaving."

14.

My Return to Paris

I WENT BACK TO PARIS, BUT IT WASN'T EASY. THE ARMY WANTED to send me back to Senegal before I was fully recovered. I was in Val-de-Grâce. The camaraderie among wounded soldiers is so important. A man who has experienced great pain recovering from surgery or has seen his wounds get worse rather than better can feel depressed, at times, in the hospital, and this is aggravated by his separation from his loved ones. You just have to listen to the men themselves, to lend an ear to the funny and irresistible trick they use to while away the unhappy hours. Here in the hospital at Val-de-Grâce the patients laugh and want everyone to laugh along with them. They don't let anyone hang on to "the blues," that little creature that wreaks havoc. The expression "Don't worry about it" ["*ne t'en fais pas*"] is always on their lips. It's a favorite with all the wounded men, even the most gravely injured. It's like a tune that everyone hums. This is because of what it means: courage and stamina in wartime. All the friendly teasing has a place, depending on the circumstances. For example, when my buddy T sees me polishing my yellow shoes, "My, my," he exclaims, "you want to change your shoe color from yellow to black?" "Yes." "You'd better put on gloves, my man." I understand what he's getting at, laugh, and show him my black hands, saying, "Don't worry about it, buddy. I've got the benefit of permanent black gloves on my hands." This makes everyone laugh.

Another time, I was looking at my friend R who was weaving a gorgeous raffia basket. I had no particular reason to look at him. I was only watching in order to learn how to make similar baskets so that, like my fellow soldiers, I could send them to my sisters. R had a thick needle like the ones used to sew up potato sacks. He threaded it with raffia. The raffia was already woven around the outside of this lovely thing. The way R held his *messallal* [needle] caught my eye: between the first two fingers of his right hand, where it didn't budge. My eyes followed the motions of that agile hand. This distracted me, and my mind, set on learning, was filled with so many thoughts inspired by my desire to make, as in a dream, little baskets of many shapes and colors in the Senegalese style. I admired the originality, the "special type." And naturally I forgot all the steps involved in making a basket, so that I had to ask my friend R to show it to me again. R had finished his basket, and he replied simply, "Ask someone else." Someone else? Who? Nobody. This is a joke invented by the patients, and it wasn't meant to be offensive. Because here, among the wounded soldiers who had been to the front, there was only one topic that would make them "bust their balls." By this, I mean, to let loose the gales of laughter a man keeps inside, clenching his stomach muscles, so that he could, without risking anything, bust a hundred and one "balls" from a hundred and two bombs. R put on a serious expression as he replied, but with all our "belly laughs," my comrades and I were able to soften him up. He dissolved in laughter, too. Suddenly in the middle of our whoops of joy, our friend G called for quiet. "Quiet down," he told us, "you're tickling the torpedo." Ha, ha, ha . . . Instead of shutting up, we howled with laughter like wolves who've eaten their fill and are baying at the moon. There are serious concerns beneath all the jokes. The soldiers enjoy talking about the years before the war. 1911, 1912, 1913 spring to our lips often, and we talk of our good life during peacetime. Each man describes what he saw, heard, and did. Young soldiers are very attached to their first love but the older ones, who've experienced the ups and downs of life and are married and the fathers of families, have a better understanding of the world and its problems, so they are more likely to mull things over than to chatter thoughtlessly. They analyze the present and the future, and things needed at home and the high cost of living dominate their conversations. I'm interested in everyone and everything they think, but I pay more attention to the elders since you must know the past in order to understand the future.

In all my memories, I distinctly recall one face among the many infantrymen I saw at Hospital 66 in Fréjus. This was the Senegalese sergeant Amidou Frama, who was killed by the Germans on the battlefield in 1918, just before the Armistice. Frama, an educated and intelligent man, thought and dreamed in French. When a black man has assimilated the customs of a country well enough to dream in that language, he's no different from a native-born Frenchman. Amidou was entirely French in his thinking. The only difference you could find between him and a Frenchman was his color, but I would be wrong to stop there: more important than the color of things or of bodies is the quality of the spirit that is the guiding light. I remember conversations we had on many topics. Frama approached them with inexhaustible integrity and honesty and had excellent analytical powers. His explanations about the French, occasionally expressed in our Senegalese language, were very simple and straightforward. He would give an example each time in order to compare one thing with another. He was especially concerned with telling our soldiers about the benefits of France's colonial regime in Africa, and he would use examples from African history when the wars between different tribes or religions destroyed the lives of the common people. Using the causes of the 1914–1918 war as an example, he enthralled his attentive listeners with his ideas about what we could expect after the war. One day, along with other soldiers, I was listening to him speak. He said, "Many of us believe people see us as no more

than hunting dogs to unleash on their prey. Oh well, that is not
true. France is too humanitarian a country to have beliefs that are
contrary to people's aspirations. To understand truly these hopes
and dreams, we must know French, which is hard even for people
who know how to read and write. The French language has so
many nuances that result in subtle differences in meaning. Still,
you can easily see what France does as a country, not as individuals.
Just as you pick through a heap of peas to keep the ones that are
good to eat and discard the pebbles, we can glean useful bits of
information from a lot of facts. Now, at this point, it's our duty to
show that we'll be worthy of France's bounty in the future." Frama
said many more things. His mind was young, lively, and as bright as
a mirror, putting a mass of things in a new light. He even reminded
me of Demba Sow, whom I hadn't seen since 1914, and who I was
still searching for. Frama explained to the soldiers the virtue of
patience that comes from willpower. He was brave and strong, and
at the same time, very sensitive in affairs of the heart. All of the
ideas he explained about all those different subjects had one goal:
harmony. He would never dispute anyone else's opinion, but he
would speak in such a way that opponents would gladly adopt his
point of view. I'm so sorry I won't see him again. With his passion,
he was one of the best advocates for humanity, and he would have
served the cause greatly by serving France.

Human beings reveal certain signs the same way that we spot
birds' heads peeping above the shelter of their nests. We usually
discern the signs of goodness, the motherlode of everything fine
in the world, less easily than signs of evil or other things: those
are more persistent and obvious. If we stick our hand in a fire,
we feel the pain and pull our hand out faster than we would from
the coldest waters. Our eyes are attracted to the sight of a red
rose because we enjoy it. We look at a burning ember because we
are curious. What is more precious than a group of agile minds

and hearts dedicated to doing good? Demba Sow would also have become an even more fervent admirer of France's generosity, if he had been here, and if he had been able to see up close the mighty France that he served. Whenever I think of these two fallen black comrades, I mourn two loyal soldiers who died for the homeland. It would have been wonderful to see them, years after the Great War, working to tap the sources of human knowledge, crystal clear and pure, holy and sweet, in full view of all people everywhere. To be sure, they left behind blood brothers, still alive, as grateful as they were, as loyal and dedicated, but these two men were precious. They could judge the significance of things they learned from experience with strict, unwavering objectivity, and they weren't afraid or too timid to express either their joys or sorrows.

15.
After the War

ONTHS WENT BY AND I HAD ALL KINDS OF PROBLEMS trying to sort out my military status. Instead of mustering out and returning to civilian life, I had to sign up for two more years. An official order enabled African soldiers who had been awarded military honors and the Croix de Guerre to become naturalized French citizens, and I believed I had the right to apply for naturalization. I also thought that as a colonial noncommissioned officer I could be reclassified as a French Army warrant officer. But in March 1920 when my rights as a citizen were affirmed by this order, I requested the pay due to me according to my rank and was told that for the civilian bureaucracy, I was a French citizen, but for the military bureaucracy, I was not. I asked to file an appeal and was sent to Marseille. There I was told to go back to Dakar! I was going to say goodbye to all my French friends and was saddened by the thought of leaving them all behind. I remembered seeing Senegalese troops leaving Menton and Saint-Raphaël to go back to the colonies, soldiers who wept because they were leaving France, despite the joyous anticipation they felt, with the prospect of seeing their black families again. They told me, when I kept asking why they were crying, that life was always wretched for us blacks. "Why do you think that?" I asked a soldier who seemed the most upset. "Why do I have to leave, maybe forever, the French here whose goodness made us love them?" That is what he said to me as a fellow soldier, and I wish I could meet him again today so that I could tell him with absolute conviction: "You're right. We are poor blacks who can't deny the feelings that link our hearts with the hearts of the people we love. We are human butterflies that people see flitting from flower to flower, from tree to tree, without knowing where our love will finally reach its destination. Whenever we want to alight on a human figure, either because it has a charming shadow or a graceful silhouette, people assume that ignorance makes us act that way and we can't appreciate the flowers' lovely perfume or the relief that shade brings when it's hot outside. Nor do they believe that we can understand the sort of human kindness that only a soul can offer a heart. Yes, we are butterflies since our love for peace, for liberty, for fraternity, and for equality makes us flit from one thing to another in our search for connection, seeking to love and be loved. But until now we haven't had the chance to be loved for our true selves. In the past, too, when we did settle down somewhere, for a long time people felt nothing more than curiosity toward us. Our skin color makes people suspicious when they don't bother looking past the surface, the exterior. However, color shouldn't mislead and blind us to the true inner essence of things and people. Everything is based on experience. Do all trees look alike? Is the earth identical to the sky in shape and color? Obviously not, and yet everything has a purpose. Yes, my friend, we are poor human butterflies. If we alight on a flower and it dries up, we'll suffer, but if it remains alive and alluring, we'll stay and love it. We've alighted on the most beautiful of all human flowers: the French soul. It neither fades nor withers away. It remains vital through the years, but, as always happens, we have no luck because we realize that by crossing the sea that separates Europe from Africa, we're forced to leave her, to leave behind French goodness and the friends we've made in the heart of France."

When, my fellow countrymen, I saw how sorry you were to leave the noble and pure hearts of the ordinary French people you've met here, just as I've done, I asked you about it. I did that to ease the pain in your heart caused by your vital connection to these European French hearts that you're leaving. I pretended to be almost ignorant of the reasons for your loyal friendships and your doubt that you could find their equal back home. I told you not to dwell on these very personal concerns just when you were leaving. Now that it's my turn to rejoin you in Africa, I feel the same regrets that you had. I would cry, if I hadn't already done so. The Frenchmen that are with you in Africa, do they have any idea how grateful you are and how powerful the memories are of the good deeds their brothers did for us in France? I doubt it, but you don't understand them well enough. Their colonial language, even when they're speaking French, doesn't have the same sound that your ears heard here and they haven't made a point of recognizing that you've come back to Africa with hearts filled with gratitude. You don't know anything about one another, like neighbors who don't spend time together. I'm telling you something I'm sure of because what I saw in the past is still true, without a doubt. You're not trying to strengthen your ties with what you learned from experience in the last war. You want to, although you're convinced that since you don't have the closeness you once had, a genuine and fraternal connection, with the French in France, there is nothing that will bring you together in genuine unity, even with the best of intentions.

Despite what the government had decided about my repatriation to Senegal, when I got to Marseille, my orders from the War Department contradicted that. So I had to take other steps, and in the meantime, the steamer that was supposed to bring me back home had left. This affected me terribly. Then I said to myself: "It's been a long time, many years, in fact, since you left your parents. They've suffered a great deal. You wanted to go back to them, to

ease their pain, and to help them now that they are old. But if you
went back to them now, with your life in flux, with your mind
distracted and upset, what kind of joy would you bring to them?
To see you again, yes of course, you are their son, and parents are
always happy to see their child again. But, alas! How will they feel
when they see how unhappy and dissatisfied you are? If you told
them about your friends, the people of France, and praised them
the way they deserved for all the goodness they extended to you
while you were in Europe, I mean, if you talked about only the
things you would rather discuss, if you obviously and deliberately
omitted all mention of the double-dealing, of the pettiness of the
military authorities' treatment of you, wouldn't your parents think
that you didn't love them any more, that your suffering was caused
merely by your regret in leaving the people of France to come
back to your parents without, in that case, really loving them? And
yet you couldn't tell them, at home, about the things that divided
human beings. You got to know France from the inside. The
military injustices you suffered were simply accidents in your life,
a thing that happens to all of us. But we have to see that against the
background of a proud and beautiful France, a generous country,
empathetic, extending to the utmost its thoughtfulness and sense
of justice to combat all the imperfections of human existence.
No, you should wait until you've settled all your business. When
everything is resolved, you'll feel calmer in your mind and lighter
in your heart. Then you can go back to your parents without any
fear and speak forthrightly about the possibilities of unity between
people, white and black, in fraternal bonds of affection."

For these reasons and others, I requested demobilization in
France, after I had found a job in Monte Carlo thanks to my good
friend Samba Diavandou. I couldn't stand to wait any longer
in the "Section," classified as partly civilian and partly military.
It certainly shouldn't have taken more than a month for the

Reform Commission to forward the details of my case to the Colonial Army Office in Paris and for the office to act on my immediate recall to my home colony under the jurisdiction of the Fifteenth Regional Command. Unfortunately, I waited for three months in Marseille for that order, and when I still hadn't received it, I decided to return to civilian life.

I understand. My case was made more complicated by the War Department itself because of the difference in ranks between the Frenchmen in the army and the native soldiers in the colonial forces, so that the Fifteenth Regional Command was itself unable to resolve the issue. It could only forward my case to the War Department for a ruling. I spent three and a half months in Monte Carlo, still waiting for a hearing, but nothing happened. It was now nine months since I had been in Paris, since I had left for the South of France, and I kept wondering when they were going to clarify my status officially. I kept on waiting. A poor man needs unlimited supplies of patience. I returned to my civilian friends in La Seine. Some of them could have helped me appeal my case, but I didn't tell them about it, and I didn't ask for anything, since their kindness was enough for me. I didn't want to spoil the charming smiles that I loved. I'll tell them all about it some day when my case is closed because then they won't feel bad about it. They'll simply understand my motives. The day after I left the service, I began working in Monte Carlo as a doorman at the Hotel National. I worked there for three and a half months with a salary that I feel bad about revealing here: sixty francs a month. It was so meager, and I had to divide it in two equal shares: one for my poor mother and the other for myself, for my health since I was worn down by mental and physical anguish.[1] When I left the hotel, I had to find a

---

1. Sixty francs a month was a very small wage in the 1920s, especially since Diallo was sending half his pay to his mother in Senegal. A loaf of bread, for example, cost three francs in 1920.

way to return to Paris and pursue the case myself; the difference
between French Army soldiers and soldiers from the colonies was
making my case more complex than ever. I was tormented by the
question of whether or not I should ask my friends for help. In any
case, there were many reasons why I went back to Paris, however
I managed it. I didn't have enough money to pay my fare. Who
could I ask for money, now that everything is so expensive and
getting more so every day? I kept asking myself this. All the ills in
the world were crushing me. My head became heavier and heavier,
my eyelids drooped down, and I couldn't keep my eyes open in the
daytime. Headaches and I don't know what else overwhelmed me
and made me depressed. And yet, all of sudden I saw my French
friends in my mind's eye. My spirits quickly rose, and in a burst
of confidence I made an impulsive decision. I went to the Post
Office and sent a telegram addressed to Marcel Perrier, 19, rue de
l'Abbé-Grégoire, Paris. I wrote: "Wire me 100 francs. Letter to
follow." The next day I left Monte Carlo to rejoin many fine French
people, like my friend Perrier. So many situations, so many chance
encounters in life, had taught me to appreciate acquaintances like
him. At a time when I was staring into the abyss, a desperate and
hopeless man, I truly understood how precious they were.

In Paris I had to find a place to live. There was a housing
shortage, unfortunately, and I didn't have enough money to pay
for lodgings—if I could find any—and also buy food until I could
count on my wages working for the Gaveau family. I ran all over
Paris for a week, asking at private houses and hotels without
finding a place. I tried to get a bed at the Black Servicemen's
hostel on Boulevard Kellerman where I had worked before as an
interpreter, but was turned down. Hotel rooms were expensive.
I scrimped a lot and ate only one meal a day so as not to have to
ask my friends for more money. The cost of living was high for
everyone and just to think of asking for a loan from one of my

acquaintances made me feel ashamed since I had no doubt they also badly needed the money. Still, when my meager resources ran out before my new job started, I had only two choices: ask someone for help or starve to death. The first option looked better to me, and I went to see Monsieur Gaveau. After I explained my problem to him, he asked his bank manager to give me fifty francs as an advance on my salary. I think I hear you scolding me, Mama Jullian, wondering why I hadn't come to you and Jullian to sit down to dinner at your table and to move back into the room I had when I was a soldier! You two dear ones were in Paris then, and I knew where to find you, but don't hold it against me, please. I didn't want you to suffer along with me. We knew each other well. I knew that your kindness and the affection you felt for me would have weighed heavily on your heart. The Gaveau family knew me also, as you know. Madame Gaveau had been one of my best nurses during the war, and when they hired me, I had the courage to ask them the favor that they granted me.

Still, since I hadn't found a room to rent, I kept looking in the best neighborhoods, because everything was full in the more modest ones. I spent an entire day on the Avenue de Wagram. I knew Madame Hasselmans had been out in the country and I decided to find out if she had come back to town. The concierge told me that she was at home, and for me, it would be both a duty and a pleasure to greet her and thank her for her past generosity. She was getting ready to go out when I arrived, but instead of leaving, she decided to stay and have a friendly chat with me. She asked if I had found a good place and naturally, I told her that a week earlier I had gotten a job with the Gaveau family and would start work on November 1. She kept on questioning me like a mother or a sister whose heart and mind, in perfect harmony, only wanted to find out everything about a son's or brother's welfare. She asked intelligent questions and gave me very sensible advice, when she judged it necessary, about my duties in the household where I had been hired because of the faith the master had in me. She also told me how I should behave. As I listened to her, I was telling myself: she is explaining what I must do: to show up at work on time every day. She didn't overlook anything and even gave me directions for the tram, bus, and Metro routes, if I needed them. She knows I'm not really used to life in Europe and a civilian job. Her knowledge and kindness enlightens me, as my own mother's would have. Having to listen carefully to a person speaking when you want to understand everything really well but at the same time are hoping for a short cut to the right answer was exhausting for me, and I almost fell asleep from the strain. I was certainly startled when Madame Hasselmans asked me, "Now, have you found a place to live?" "No, madame, I've been looking for a room since I got here, in hotels, in private homes, but I haven't found anything. I'm a victim of the housing crisis!" "Don't look any further. I have a spare room. I'll let you have it." "Ah, thank you so much, madame!" "Just give me a minute, please, and I'll get the key and show it to you." Once we were inside the room, she showed me the paintings on the walls. There were portraits of great masters, writers, artists, and musicians. Among them I read the name "L. van Beethoven." There were also photographs she had taken of Monaco, Monte Carlo, and other magnificent places she had visited. My gaze rested on an armoire standing to the left of the entrance and this caught my benefactor's attention. She said immediately, in a maternal tone: "You can put your things in there. Here, you see, you can hang your clothes. Take care not to break the glass. That's expensive nowadays!" She smiled charmingly as she looked at me. It occurred to me that I should take advantage of the "high cost of living" to find out exactly what motivated Madame Hasselmans's generosity toward me. I still remembered what she had told me in 1921 after her friend's brother, Captain Coste, had died. That explained why she wanted to help me, but I wanted to explore the question a bit further to find out, at the very least, how clearly she remembered my captain. "It's true, Madame. Everything is very expensive. That's one of the effects of the war. I've always been very grateful for your help when I needed to find work, but now, well, I wouldn't be able to stay in a hotel without paying. Will you let me to pay something for this room every month, even if it's only sixty-five francs?" "No, absolutely not, my poor Bakary. I don't want it. If your dear departed Captain Coste had lived, he would have done the same for you without expecting payment or anything else from you. As for me, it's a nice way to honor his memory and demonstrate my friendship for his sister, who first sent you to me."

You see, Mama Jullian, your good intentions have inspired others to good deeds, including the one today. You once told me: "In France, the children of our French colonies should be treated in the same way they treat their own families in Africa, with sweet, loving devotion." You wanted to take my mother's place, and Madame Hasselmans's generosity has replaced the kindness of my former captain, who died in service to France. I have already described many kind French hearts whom I met. There are others whom my black brothers have known and loved, people who joined you, Mama Jullian, in the great, humanistic work of demonstrating to everyone you meet how we can love each other without caring about skin color. Today I can't stop thinking about it. Sometimes in the past I would be preoccupied with things that I didn't know or that I hadn't had time to examine deeply. *Essi, hûndé*—but nowadays I understand these things. I have a full life, filled to overflowing with goodness, that essential quality that is both human and divine.

I think about my godmother and her family, the Baudrys. It seems to me that I'm always surrounded by this family and their friends and relations, as I was in December 1916 during one of the leaves I spent in Cette. This was the first leave I had gotten from the hospital, and the directors let me go in the hopes it would change my mental state, which was oppressed by my wounds, my pain, and my loneliness. During my time in Cette, people gathered around my miserable self, smiled at me, spoke to me kindly, asked me if I needed anything, if I was hungry or thirsty. They talked about my black brothers, told me how much they appreciated them, how they loved them. They asked me about my Senegalese family, about my mother. They left work or spent a day off showing me France in all the attractions of their town: a statue, a monument, a museum, an impressive commercial building, an antique painting. They stopped everywhere and explained everything to me. They introduced me, with the highest praise, to every friend they met. At the end of the day, after dinner and the charming conversation that followed, they hugged me. "Good night! Tomorrow at nine, you'll have breakfast in bed!"

I thought of Montpellier. I had a leave there and stayed with my beloved Dufour family. Etienne, the father, was an architect. Someone is knocking at the door: "Come in!" "Good morning Bakary! Did you sleep well?" A smile, a kiss, a cup of hot coffee with breakfast after I get out of the bed whose softness makes me a slugabed. We're going to see the Vitou family. Here they are, very friendly. We exchange kisses, are introduced to friends, lovely friends. I don't know exactly why, but for me, I associate my friend Etienne Dufour's name with the essence of goodness and the kind of tact that attracts everyone. I know this comparison is especially apt. Etienne Dufour is a fearless man, cheerful, friendly, with an artistic temperament, always ready to be helpful. Madame Juliette Dufour is my second godmother since she is Madame Baudry's, my original godmother's, cousin. She is as kind as her husband. When two people share an understanding and live together in harmony, they end up resembling each other in spirit.

And here's Gaston Joseph Jullian and his family in Paris: "How are you, Diallo? I don't want you to have any more operations," Mama Jullian said as she hugged me. "*No more. You're fine as you are. Think about your poor mother in Senegal. She needs to see you again.*" My friend Jullian hugged me next, gave me a hearty handshake, and added: "Your Mama Jullian is right. Don't agree to have another operation after the thirteenth one. Now all you need to do is to rest up and to recover your strength." After having coffee or tea, lunch or dinner, my friend Jullian, who was always instinctively kind, chose a topic of conversation at random—stories, anecdotes, et cetera. He taught me good French pronunciation. We would spend one, two, or three hours together, and talk the whole time. He had a booming voice, as powerful as his mind, and just as inexhaustible as his desire to teach me. Mama Jullian would listen to us talking and smile at us from time to time. I was thinking just yesterday that the soul of Mama Marie Jullian is the very picture of French goodness. I still think so today. She never cursed or expresssed vulgar thoughts. She only said pleasant things that you wouldn't mind saying yourself.

I think about the Henri Corlieu family. Hearty kisses for everyone. "How are you feeling?" asks my adopted father as soon as I arrive. Everyone gathers around me! Warm feelings, always affectionate! "Goodbye, Diallo. See you soon. Come to lunch tomorrow." "Goodbye, papa. Goodbye, mama. Goodbye, Henriette!" The doorbell rings. Someone comes to the door. "Look, it's Diallo!" "Good morning, Germaine. Good morning, papa. Good morning, mama." They gather round. We talk about France and its colonies. They talk about my Senegalese comrades. Kind words, affectionate smiles. They ask me if I've heard from my parents. "Have a cup of coffee, Diallo, and let's make a toast to your family's health, so far away."

Goodness. "I'm sorry to leave so soon, but it's time to go back to the hospital." "Goodbye, Diallo. Come and see us again soon. We always enjoy it." Warm handshakes. I think of all the French Red Cross nurses who cared for me. I think of all my French friends! The Madon de Colombes family! What a collection of kind hearts! "Dear Monsieur Bakary, we'd be very glad if you could spend next Sunday with us." Wonderful memories are contained in those words, to be repeated from one Sunday to the next, and always I think of Monsieur Valentin Bain, the government inspector for primary schools in Manosque (Basses-Alpes) who, when I first arrived in that town, realized that I was lost and that I didn't know how to reach my good friend Collignon at the Château de Barême. He left his friends, came up to me, and said: "The town is a little far from the station. If you are going there, would you like to come in the car with us?" I'll always remember the expression of tactful kindness on his face. And you two, Madame and Monsieur Charles Poggi from Marseille: Why wouldn't I still be thinking of you just as I never stop thinking about my black comrades whom you so enjoyed inviting to your home? Just as I remember the friendly Raspail family in your city? The Countess André de Berthier de Sauvigny, the director of nursing volunteers for the wounded soldiers at the Val-de-Grâce hospital in Paris: I think of you every time I happen to think about the good deeds of generous France, especially when I think of Madame Gaveau, Mademoiselle Lozé, Mademoiselle Sevaistre, Mademoiselle Pelletier, Madame Le Drogo, and so many others. I think of you, the A. Richard family, you who said such fine things about black people whom you knew wanted to love you as we did sincerely. Ah! Monsieur Jean-Richard Bloch,[2] you so ably communicate your fine, intelligent feelings

---

2. Jean-Richard Bloch (1884–1947) was a French writer and political activist. He helped Diallo publish *Force-Bonté*.

for humanity to everyone. How you prove that the birth of true brotherhood among men is unstoppable, inevitable!

I think of all those who showed, even if only for one second, a spirit of generosity toward my miserable self, as you did for my poor African brothers. And thinking of all of you, men and women of France, thinking about the wonderful things you gave us during and after the Great War, I feel truly glad that I replaced my shepherd's staff with a pen and my flock with your noble sense of justice. I didn't want to remain a shepherd, but then, persuaded by the force of your goodness, I asked you to make me a Shepherd of Gratitude. You would have wanted it that way, Your Ladyship, the Honorable Lucie Cousturier,[3] whose humane temperament inspired your independent soul to the utmost development of common sense, toward goodness, toward humanity; goodness and humanity, you understood them in the broadest sense. You tried so hard to resolve the problems in which self-interest has ensnared human hearts who only aspire to be good. I think of all the French, bar none, all the decent folks my Senegalese brothers described, my comrades who, like me, had the opportunity during their time in France to glimpse the French soul. Your generosity was intended for us Senegalese, the troops that I had the honor to shepherd. Only the people who didn't get a chance to know you well couldn't freely and easily allow their hearts to love you. Your good humor couldn't fail to charm everyone who met you, because it always came with a smile, a smile that was like the sunlight, if I can put this into words, like the inner light that one feels deep inside: goodness!

I saw you during wartime and during peacetime. I observed you from morning till night, under all sort of circumstances, during

---

3. Lucie Cousturier (1876–1925) was a French painter and writer. During World War I she organized a school in her home to teach French to African soldiers. She assisted Diallo in preparing the manuscript for *Force-Bonté*.

those times. Your nurses and doctors working with the wounded, your troops and ours, never made even the least distinction between their patients. I saw at close range thousands of your people do good deeds: civilians—men, women, and children—performing extremely generous acts, demonstrating the openhandedness that is characteristic of you, and among you, I saw poor people who rivaled the rich with their kindness, loyalty, and generosity, toward us and toward all. You changed me, I swear it, my head, my heart, my mind, and my soul. I don't want to hide this from you now. In the past, I was filled with false ideas about you. I was told that you were bad people. I was afraid of you, and when you fear people, you run away from them. But chance brought us together and this close contact led to understanding. I love you. My fellow soldiers who got to know you well love you, too, and we'll do everything in our power to make our families love you, too. They'll love you. Young black men and women will benefit the most from knowing you. This is the most important point, because in Africa their fathers, each in turn, say, as is customary, "The friends of my children are my friends." These children are the black soldiers you called to fight in the war. There are many among them who are buried in French soil, and their graves represent a serious moral guarantee. May those guarantees remain in force! Let's all work together without any racial divisions. Color is on the outside, and we know that we are profoundly affected by goodness inside our bodies and cruelty only on the outside. Let's all love each other, despite the superficial prejudices meant to keep us apart. Everything has a purpose. Let's try to find the purposes that will unite us forever!

In the lovely Parc Monceau in Paris, I see birds looking for food. They peck at the manicured green lawns with their beaks, one, two, three times, and more, in the same spot, and they turn their heads, to the left and to the right, and their feeble cries of "Tui . . . tui . . . ," make them resemble hungry children even more. God Almighty! The wind shakes the trees and rattles the branches. You might say the trees are trying to start walking. A young, blonde, pretty woman has just arrived. She watches the birds and crumbles her bread into bits to give to them, these cute little birds flexing their wings, who hop toward her. Are they going to eat from her hand?

"Cui . . . cui . . . cui . . ." What are they saying now? Is it "thanks, thanks, thanks"? There's no doubt they understand the lady's generosity because now they're crowding around her feet. They would have fled if she was holding a stick, a gun, a rock, or an arrow to aim at them. Opposite her, a spray of water from the fountain rises to the sky and then falls like a shower of rain on the circular bed of flowers around it. The lady is still feeding her bread to the birds flocking around her. Ah! It's a lovely sight. To me, the birds are like us, the black people who want to love, and that lady is France! Grateful birds, you know how to show your happiness to everyone enjoying the fresh air. Your little "cui . . . cui . . ." sounds mean that you can speak. Anyone who is paying attention to you can see how much you value the hearts who take care of you. Sitting opposite your benefactor, this lady with a charming face, with golden blond hair, who thought of your needs when sharing her bread, I ask you to say along with me: "Long live France's strength and goodness!"

The Rape of a Country

✠

Lamine Senghor

1.

The Pale Man

O NCE UPON A TIME, IN A FARAWAY LAND ON THE SAVANNA in the back of beyond, near a river whose banks were lined with lush green trees, where the reflections of the leaves tinted the water a bluish green all along the waterway, there was a house made of wood, reeds, straw, and tree bark. A family lived inside the house: a wise old man, his wives, and their children.

This family lived together in perfect harmony. A brother almost never complained about his sister, nor a sister about her brother. You rarely heard anyone, except for babies, crying. You could say that if there hadn't been little spats sometimes between the many wives of this poor old man, who resented the favoritism their husband occasionally showed to one or another, this house would really have earned the name the old fellow wanted so optimistically to give it: "*M'Bine Diam*"—the house of peace—because it contained everything they needed to live happily and peacefully.

But one day the children were swimming in the river and caught sight of a boat landing near their village. They ran home to tell the rest of the family. Everyone wanted to know what was going on. The ones who could go, ran to the village, leaving the others at home. But when they got closer to the riverbank, they saw a very frightening sight—the man who was climbing out of the boat had such a pale face that it looked like the skin of a plucked chicken. Besides that, under his nostrils and above his upper lip there were hairs so long that they looked like the feathers hanging from a quill pen. And to top it all off, the "pale face" had no beard.

167

Can you believe it? No, never, not in a million years! These poor folks had never seen a person this color. They couldn't even imagine that human beings would have a skin color other than ebony or mahogany. At the sight of such a pale face with an upper lip sprouting such long hairs, curled up into two points on either side of his nostrils, like the horns on a cow's head, the children ran away, the adults stood watching at a safe distance . . . with wary looks, their curiosity piqued, they examined this extremely pale and abominably hairy man.

This most unusual traveler waved his hand, inviting them to come closer. The bravest ones did. He tried hard to make them understand, with gestures and a language that sounded like the "cathios-cothios" (a kind of canary but colored a brighter shade of yellow and even more talkative than ordinary canary birds) that he had brought lovely trinkets for them from his native land, things that would bedazzle them, and that he would trade for goods from their country that he would pick out.

They were eager to see the treasures their guest described, curious to take a closer look at things that came from a land of such pale-skinned people. So they nodded to show that they agreed, mostly without understanding what the trader was saying. Noticing that they were eager to see his goods, the paleface unloaded all sorts of knickknacks of various colors from the boat to show the crowd gathered around him.

The fear (that weak-minded people in the countryside feel the first time they meet a person of an unexpected color) melted away and those who originally hadn't dared come close to the "paleface" approached him. Little by little, a crowd gathered around the man who had so frightened them. If you had seen them from a distance, you would have thought they looked like vultures feeding on corpses, the victims of an imperialist army on an African battlefield.

The paleface unwrapped bottles, boots, bags, strips of leather, carved bits of wood, et cetera. There were goods from the bric-a-brac shop, the grocer, the butcher, the fabric shop, and the corner store, but most of his wares came from the distillery and the firearms factory. The pharmacist, the bookseller, and . . . *humanity* hadn't, seemingly by accident, supplied anything to the traveling salesman.

At that time, in that country, people didn't do anything without consulting their elders. This rule of natural law in their land meant that they had to ask their guest to come with them and consult the men with long white beards and show his wares to the elders who hadn't ventured outside their homes.

They were able to explain this to the merchant using these gestures: "to look at" (pointing at an eye) and "long beards" (pretending to stroke a long beard with one hand while touching a white object with the other). He bundled up his goods and then followed his customers toward the village, which was actually one house, an agglomeration of round huts encircling a shared courtyard.

After he arrived at the house and was helped to open his packs and display his wares, the paleface uncorked some bottles and served drinks to the elders; he opened some jars and gave everyone a taste of their contents.

Since in that land no one knew what buying and selling meant, the village chief gave an order—that the paleface be escorted into the huts, storehouses, grain lofts, stables, backyards, flocks, and fields; that he even be given gold dust and anything else that caught his eye. He was escorted all around; he was invited into the storehouses, huts, fields, among the flocks, in the stables, and everywhere that contained objects of interest. The paleface poked, pinched, and squeezed, handled everything within his reach, grabbed whatever he liked!

Never before had a trader come upon such a bounty! He piled up elephant tusks, the pelts and claws of wild animals, and also cattle, chickens, and goats, fruits, jewelry made of gold and silver, and even a fair amount of gold dust.

After he finished picking and choosing his treasure trove, the villagers helped him load the goods onto his boat. When it was packed so full that there was not an inch of empty space left, the paleface, with a very heavy heart, had to leave some things behind.

The villagers invited the lucky trader to spend a little more time with them, to eat with them in their house. The trader understood immediately when he saw one man gesturing, bringing his hand up to his mouth, so he followed them. As soon as he stepped inside, he was invited to sit on a mat, and was served couscous with meat to eat and milk to drink. He ate a great deal but hardly drank at all!

The people danced, sang, and above all drank until very late that night. Because the paleface realized he had succeeded in his mission beyond his wildest dreams, he let the villagers know that he wanted to go back to his boat and sleep, so that he could leave with the morning tide, when the roosters crowed cock-a-doodle-doo.

The elderly chief decreed that the celebration was over. Everything stopped, just like that. He ordered one of his sons to accompany their guest back to his boat. After giving the traveler ceremonial salutes and wishes for a good journey, the villagers returned to their huts. Dégou Diagne, armed with a lance balanced on his shoulder, escorted the paleface to the river bank.[1]

---

1. Lamine Senghor names his villainous African character Diagne after Blaise Diagne, the Senegalese representative in the French Chamber of Deputies. Senghor despised Diagne as a collaborator with French colonial rule, and he condemned him for recruiting African soldiers to fight in World War I. See Introduction, pp. 11–12.

The School of Crime

As they walked, the foreigner said to Dégou Diagne, "I have a good luck charm that I will give you if you aren't afraid to do what I ask."

"I fear nothing, you understand, and that's why my father chose me, and only me, to escort you to the riverside."

"Here's what I want," the paleface told him, "I want you, tomorrow morning before the sun is high in the sky, to bring me one of your brothers in exchange for this charm. I will wait for you down along the bend in the river. I'll tie up my boat there."

Dégou Diagne shuddered as he heard the paleface making this awful offer! But the man added: "The charm I'm going to give you is worth more than a little boy!!! If you knew its value, you wouldn't hesitate to accept my offer. Just imagine! You will be the only man in this entire country to own one of these! With this charm you won't need a lance to defend yourself against wild animals or the enemies who want to harm you. I'll tell you the secret when you bring me the boy, but you have to swear that you will do it, so that I'll wait for you over there, where no one will see us."

The pride he would feel in owning a charm that no one else in the whole country had, and the enthralling persuasiveness of this man who couldn't even speak Dégou Diagne's language, had an overwhelming effect on his mind and succeeded in winning him over. Dégou Diagne accepted the paleface's offer. They said goodbye and arranged to meet the next day at the bend in the river. When Dégou Diagne got back to the village, everyone was already asleep. He lay down but he couldn't sleep because of the nightmares his bargain with the paleface gave him.

He got up a bit later than usual; after breakfast he asked two of his brothers to go with him to gather wood, saying they needed the branches to repair two sections of his mother's house. They walked toward the river, around the bend where he claimed to have once seen some excellent branches. The sun was already climbing high in the sky when they came to the spot the two accomplices had chosen. The paleface with the hairy mouth was waiting for them there. Dégou Diagne exclaimed with a feigned air of surprise: "Look, it's the boat of the man who visited us yesterday. Maybe he is resting after the busy day. Let's go and see him for a little while." Having heard their voices, the paleface looked up and recognized his accomplice from the night before. He left his boat and came on shore, walking toward Dégou Diagne. He was holding a tool, about three hands in length, made of wood and iron. In his other hand, he held a box and a little sack made of gray canvas.

He took his accomplice aside, gave him the charm, a box of mysterious black powder, and the sack of small iron balls. He explained how to use the charm. A few minutes later, Dégou Diagne gestured toward his brothers and asked the trader to point out which one he wanted. When they heard these words, the two boys got scared and tried to run away, but the paleface had already grabbed one of them and tied him up. Seeing this, the other boy tried to run back to the village and spread the news about the crime. Afraid of being accused, Dégou Diagne took this opportunity to use his new charm. He aimed at his brother and fired the weapon the way the paleface had just showed him, squeezing the little tongue on the underside of the charm. A huge bang was heard, a boom that echoed through the woods . . . boom . . . mmm . . . mmm! The charm had spit out iron, fire, and smoke on the boy running away.

Holes piercing his spine and his skull, the boy lay flat on the ground, lifeless, struck down so brutally that you would have thought he'd been hit by lightning. Dégou Diagne's criminal tutorial had begun getting results!

The Assassin's Lie

To cover up their crime, with the paleface's help Dégou Diagne buried the brother he had killed. After this self-serving and nonhumanitarian burial, the partners in crime said farewell to each other at the grave that would be an everlasting testament to their murderous act. One man left on his boat, gliding on the current, taking with him a boy torn away from the people he loved the most in the world. A brother's betrayal! The captive mourned in his heart for the boy who was killed and the family he would never see again!!! At the same time, the other man brought a double dose of grief to his family's house, which he himself provoked by betraying his brothers. With the hypocritical look of a murderer on his face, he returned home without any wood, with no tools, no brothers, but with a corrupt mind, stuffed with falsehoods that he had learned from the paleface's schooling. His eyes were brimming with crocodile tears while his murderous mind was inventing an incredible tale to explain the disappearance of his brothers.

His father saw him return with a mournful expression on his face and asked at once: "Dégou Diagne, what happened? Why are you coming back alone and so sad?"

"Father! You must have heard a little while ago, that loud bang? It sounded like thunder!"

"Why yes," his father replied. "I was actually surprised to hear thunder in the middle of the dry season, and I couldn't understand what made the echo I heard." (The old man had never heard a gunshot.)

"Ah, well, Father, that awful noise came out of a monster's mouth, a creature I've never seen before. It was bigger than a horse and twice as heavy as a bull. It had four legs, two wings, a mouth like a serpent, but three times bigger than a crocodile's maw!!! We were gathering wood to repair my mother's house, which is getting rickety, when this creature seized my two brothers who were thirty feet away from me. It tucked one boy under each wing and flew off making that terrible squawk! I hid beneath a tree, watching its eyes swiveling in their sockets, eyes that blazed red like fire. My brothers were screaming from underneath its wings, which seemed to have claws to hold them fast. It flew toward the water. I didn't come out of my hiding place until it was no longer visible in the sky!"

This tissue of lies that the entire family heard, trembling with emotion, stunned their hearts and they all began to cry, and the killer sobbed along with them! . . . All day and all night, their mothers wept hot tears, as did the father. The killer conducted the weeping orchestra. Three days after they disappeared, the people offered the usual ritual prayers at the altars of their gods, and conducted a ceremony in their honor. The year of their death acquired two nicknames: the year of the paleface and the year of the monster.

X

Happiness for One Person, Sadness for the Other

THE PALE MAN RETURNED HOME WITH HIS BOAT LOADED WITH treasures. He unloaded the most valuable things and secretly smuggled on shore a little boy whose skin was ebony colored. (Nice!) The pale man, called "Bourgeois" by his countrymen, was quite proud of his accomplishments and boasted about the success of his trip.[2] All around the country people competed to invite Master Bourgeois to dinner or to be his guest in order to hear about his exploits and gawk at his ebony-colored slave. His trip provoked his compatriots' sense of adventure and prideful vanity to such an extent that some of them formed a corporation to send out several boats on an expedition the following year!!!

As for Dégou Diagne, he felt the weight of his brothers' betrayal and murder in the magic rifle slung over his shoulder. *This was the beginning of trade, of all kinds of importing and exporting, between these countries and these different races.*

---

2. As a communist, Senghor names his white villain Bourgeois. In the writings of Karl Marx, the founder of modern communism, the bourgeoisie is the class of capitalist exploiters.

2.

Conquest

The Invasion

THE FOLLOWING YEAR AROUND THE SAME TIME, THREE BIG SHIPS arrived in the country. Many men disembarked. They were the same color as the one who had come the year before. The paleface led the men to the village. When they arrived, everyone came outside to take a look at them and their goods. The chief approached the strangers, welcomed them, and then declared the market open.

While some of the pale foreigners traded their wares with the villagers, three other palefaces, dressed in long black robes with long tails trailing down one side, balancing flat black hats that looked like plates on their heads, assembled a group of young men and began teaching them the art of fratricide.[1] Dégou Diagne, who had already been poisoned with Satan's beliefs, acted as their interpreter. Here was a man who had proved his worth!!!

The merchants were able to finish all their trading before nightfall and loaded up their ships with their bounty. That evening the villagers didn't invite the visitors to come and dance; it was the other way around—the foreigners invited the villagers to spend an evening of fun with them on board their ships. An orchestra was playing on each boat. The villagers climbed into canoes that would take them to the ships anchored along the shore. The sounds of accordions wheezing and trumpets blaring deafened everyone on

---

1. Senghor is describing the traditional costume worn by Catholic priests.

board. Liquor was poured generously into the cups of anyone who wanted it. Everyone's desires were satisfied on deck and inside the cabins. In the meantime, young people, half drunk, climbed down into the holds where they sold their brothers and sisters for a magic charm that would spit fire and a handful of little iron balls that would bring down man and beast.

The next morning before the sun came up the ships set sail, carrying away their bounty, the fruits of their trading during the day and the festivities at night . . . a criminal and degenerate enterprise above all!

Ж

The Reign of King Colonialism

TWO YEARS LATER, SEVERAL SHIPS RETURNED TO THE COUNTRY, but since the country folk refused absolutely to listen to what the strangers said or to look at what they wanted to show them, the palefaces went on the attack. The country folk fought back courageously. But they had to surrender to the powerful, criminal weapons that the enemy used against them. After a fierce and long resistance, the country folk realized that their enemies' weapons were more "civilized" than theirs, and they acknowledged their defeat.

That's when they spotted the paleface, Master Bourgeois, the former trader, who had returned to their land dressed in a general's uniform and was now having himself declared king. They understood what had happened . . . and he took the name "King Colonialism." From that day on, their plots of land, their fields, their flocks, and their freedom no longer belonged to them. They had once been free but they became enslaved people. "We have to civilize you!" the paleface proclaimed. He was now their master, their Lord and Master.

Expanding the Conquest

SINCE KING COLONIALISM'S REALM WAS NOT AS VAST AS HIS ambition, he armed his slaves and forced them to conquer neighboring territories in his name. This is how King Colonialism managed to expand his realm and end up ruling over an empire that was bigger than his own home country.[2] A year later ships commanded by another equally ambitious man, just as pale as the newly crowned Lord and Master, came to attack his empire and wrested it away from him. A few years later, the deposed leader marshaled his forces and retook the kingdom he had lost. He too was the target of a number of attacks by men of his same color and race, and this motivated him to sign treaties with his enemies in order to maintain his status as king. These treaties gave each bandit the right to declare himself the leader of that slice of territory that he had conquered.[3] And this is how the invasion of these "virgin lands" took place, in the home of the innocents who had no "civilized weapons"!

The innocents were reduced to absolute slavery. They were sold to anyone who wanted to buy them. And through trade it was even possible to repopulate islands previously home to people whose skin was more red than rosy.[4] And these red island dwellers

---

2. Senghor is describing France's use of African soldiers, the *Tirailleurs Sénégalais*, to conquer more territory for the French colonial empire.

3. This refers to the eighteenth-century colonial wars in which European nations like Britain and France seized African territory for themselves.

4. This refers to the extermination of Native Americans and the creation of the African slave trade to provide labor for France's colonies in the Caribbean.

were exterminated by the palefaces when they fought against the invasion, resisting to the very last man. (Exemplary!)

Nevertheless, after a long and fierce struggle the humanitarian feelings of a few great men succeeded in abolishing the shameful practice of buying and selling human beings of whatever color.[5] For a while people lived in peace, and there was no more talk of war except in the white men's countries.

5. This refers to the abolition of slavery. France finally abolished slavery in its overseas colonies in 1848.

3.

The White Queen

The War in the Heart of the Kingdom

AFTER THE EMPEROR IN KING COLONIALISM'S NATIVE COUNTRY was assassinated by rebellious citizens, he was replaced by the sister of the deceased king and mother of King Colonialism. In order to tighten their hold on power the mother and son united their two kingdoms into one single empire, despite the great distance separating them.[1] The Queen Republic reigned over the citizens at home, while the King Colonialism governed the subjects in their territories abroad.

One fine day one of the king's brothers, Germain Bourgeois, was overwhelmed with jealousy and demanded the queen cede to him the overseas territory next to hers. Some of the officers in the White Queen's court argued against it, saying that King Germain had stolen two important properties from the deceased monarch over a period of forty months.[2]

The queen's prime minister, knowing full well that her army could not win a war against her brother King Germain, explained to the generals and officers that it would be better to make concessions than to wage war against King Germain. The prime

---

1. This refers to the overthrow of French emperor Napoleon III in 1870 and the creation of a French Republic. Senghor emphasizes the irony of a democratic nation (France) maintaining a despotic rule over its African colonies.

2. This passage alludes to France's loss of the provinces of Alsace and Lorraine ("two important properties") to Germany ("Bourgeois Germain") during the Franco-Prussian War of 1870. Germany was also trying to expand its control over African territory at the expense of France.

minister managed to persuade the queen to cede a few territories of her "other people's lands" to her brother, whose burning ambition to grow and grow infected all the kings around him.

Everyone thought at that time that the queen's concession would put an end to the threats of a disastrous war. False hopes! Two months later, her brother Germain found an excuse, which to this day no one has understood, to attack the queen inside her own borders (or, rather, the queen, the king, and their ministers found a way to fight a war risking their subjects' necks, not their own).[3]

The other small countries surrounding the queen's and King Germain's lands were quite familiar with Germain's ambitions, so they rushed to help the queen, fearing that if she was defeated in the war, they would be invaded next.

To reinforce her army the queen called on King Colonialism's subjects, promising to do away with the pernicious laws of modernized slavery that she had imposed on their country. Now they would be recognized as full-fledged citizens of her own land, equal to those with whom they stood shoulder to shoulder, defending the rights and freedoms of people to determine their own future.[4]

Some were profoundly moved by her lovely words and enlisted in the military. But most of King Colonialism's subjects scoffed at the queen's claims, saying that her and her son's promises had never been fulfilled, and because of this they couldn't take seriously what she had just told them. In any case, they argued, this war was a family quarrel, so there was absolutely no reason for slaves to get involved on one side or the other.

---

3. This refers to the start of World War I. Unlike Bakary Diallo, who represents France's war aims as democratic and progressive, Senghor sees the war as a selfish grab for land by the ruling class who callously sacrifice the lives of the poor.

4. Here Senghor refers to France's recruiting propaganda in Africa, which promises Africans enhanced rights in return for their wartime service.

Since the queen's army needed more cannon fodder, she had to take stricter measures with King Colonialism's subjects. They were conscripted by force. But the roundup didn't bring in enough recruits, and the queen tried another tactic: diplomacy backed up by the forces of order. She sent her most loyal slave with ebony-colored skin to persuade his brothers, using fine words, to join the National Defense Force and fight several thousands of miles away from their homeland.[5]

This good fellow was escorted by a squad of uniformed soldiers of his own race, wearing officers' stripes, their chests dripping with medals. He set off for his former homeland one fine day surrounded by lieutenants and corporals with white faces. He gave the mission his all, speechifying eloquently. But since he didn't talk in their native language, you can just imagine the effect his harangues in the "white man's" tongue had on his ebony-colored audiences, even though a brother was speaking.

After these speeches that no one understood, which had to be translated more or less by the interpreters, who were lower ranking slaves with the stench of gunpowder in their nostrils, King Colonialism's subjects took to their heels and fled. And the loyal ebony-colored patriot who had been recruited by his beloved queen hunted down thousands of his brothers hiding in the woods.

This disgusted even some of the palefaces who would rather sacrifice themselves in battle than force unwilling conscript-captives to go and die for a cause they knew nothing about, to sacrifice for hollow false promises.

The fighting continued for three months, with thousands injured or killed. Still, one day victory was declared for the queen and her allies. The queen regained the properties that King Germain had

5. This refers to Blaise Diagne's recruitment mission to West Africa in 1918. See Introduction, p. 15.

won from the previous king and she and her allies divvied up the lands he had stolen abroad.[6] Then, as King Germain and his family had fled far, far away, a queen was enthroned in his place, Queen Germaine.

---

6. France regains Alsace and Lorraine, and France and Great Britain take over Germany's African colonies.

4.

The Revolution

After the Armistice

AFTER THE VICTORY THAT HAD BEEN SO LONG ANTICIPATED BY
people of all colors in every country, the slaves reminded the
queen of the promises made during the recruitment drive. Their
efforts were in vain. The queen informed them that not only
was she unable to fulfill those promises, but that all her subjects,
whether they were dark-skinned, white, or yellow, would have to
be penalized—by doubling their taxes, by having them work more
for less pay, by having to buy food at higher prices, pay higher rent,
and eat less!!!¹ This was because the queen's former allies wanted
to be compensated for their wartime contributions even though
she was completely bankrupted by the costs of war, and the new
queen who ascended to King Germain's throne wasn't inclined to
pay the indemnity required.

𝕏

The Revolt

THE SLAVE EXPLOITATION SYSTEM BECAME TWICE AS TOUGH FOR
the dark-skinned people; the yellow skins suffered the same.
But alcohol and opium production were also doubled as the

---

1. Here Senghor refers to France's broken promises to Africans of greater self-
government after the war. Instead, colonized peoples have to endure higher taxes to
pay off France's war debts.

forced intake of these poisons and the resulting deaths increased everywhere. The paleface citizens were brought to their knees by poverty, starvation, and tuberculosis infections brought on by exhaustion, by overwork and hunger, by living in hovels, having to dress in rags.

Everyone was angry. The fury grew . . . grew . . . and grew until one day the paleface citizens who wanted to rise up against their queen realized that they would have to enlist fellow slaves in their revolt. Otherwise, the defenders of "the crown" would recruit them to serve as counterrevolutionaries. So, they sent emissaries to all the enslaved lands to organize revolts by showing them how much they had been cheated and looted, by telling them that the queen recognized differences between people because of their color, not their worth. They informed them that, despite their own pitiful condition, the queen had immiserated the palefaces less than the others. "You know," they said, "your war wounded are paid by the queen only a sixth of what ours are, for the same injury, the same amputation, the same illness. The widows of our fallen fellow soldiers, their orphan children are paid, while the wives and children of your fallen comrades get nothing from the paymasters![2] . . . You realize that you ought to be the first to rebel, instead of acting as counterrevolutionaries defending a queen who has broken all her promises. Your brothers who are suffering are giving you the choice to decide for yourselves."

Everyone saw the truth of these words and recognized where their duty lay. In the village squares, anger grew ever more intense. It rose . . . and rose some more! It reached such a pitch that one fine morning (Friday the 13th) it exploded. The very same day, at the same time, dark-skins, yellow-skins, and the "less white"

---

2. African war veterans who fought for France were paid far less than white French soldiers.

rose up in revolt along with the paleface citizens who were the native-born subjects of the queen. Rulers were overturned, the queen was sent to dive for pearls in the deep ocean void, and King Colonialism was delivered to the tender mercies of the angel of death. The sun rose and it was the Day of Liberation.

The slaves were free! The citizens in every country participated in their own government. Together, they made a pact of free nations. LONG LIVE THE REVOLUTION!!!

Further Reading

Balesi, Charles John. *From Adversaries to Comrades-in-Arms: West Africans and the French Military, 1885–1918*. Waltham, MA: Crossroads, 1979.

Boittin, Jennifer Anne. *Colonial Metropolis: The Urban Grounds of Anti-Imperialism and Feminism in Interwar Paris*. Lincoln: University of Nebraska Press, 2010.

Conklin, Alice L. *A Mission to Civilize: The Republican Ideas of Empire in France and West Africa*. Stanford, CA: Stanford University Press, 1997.

Echenberg, Myron. *Colonial Conscripts: The Tirailleurs Sénégalais in French West Africa, 1857–1960*. Portsmouth, NH: Heinemann, 1991.

Fogarty, Richard S. *Race and War in France: Colonial Subjects in the French Army, 1914–1918*. Baltimore: Johns Hopkins University Press, 2008.

Johnson, G. Wesley. *The Emergence of Black Politics in Senegal: The Struggle for Power in the Four Communes, 1900–1920*. Stanford, CA: Stanford University Press, 1971.

Likosky, Stephan. *With a Weapon and a Grin: Postcard Images of France's Black African Colonial Troops in WWI*. Atglen, PA: Schiffer Publishing, 2017.

Lunn, Joe. *Memoirs of the Maelstrom: A Senegalese Oral History of the First World War*. Portsmouth, NH: Heinemann, 1999.

Mann, Gregory. *Native Sons: West African Veterans and France in the Twentieth Century*. Durham, NC: Duke University Press, 2006.

Moyd, Michelle. "Centring a Sideshow: Local Experiences of the First World War in Africa." *First World War Studies* 7 (2016): 111–30.

Murphy, David. "Defending the 'Negro Race': Lamine Senghor and Black Internationalism in Interwar France." *French Cultural Studies* 24, no. 2 (2013): 161–73.

Parsons, Timothy. "Mobilising Africa's Empire for War: Pragmatism vs. Trusteeship." *Journal of Modern European History* 13, no. 2 (2015): 183–202.

Strachan, Hew. *The First World War in Africa*. Oxford: Oxford University Press, 2004.

Zimmerman, Sarah. "*Mesdames Tirailleurs* and Indirect Clients: West African Women and the French Colonial Army, 1908–1918." *International Journal of African Historical Studies* 44, no. 2 (2011): 299–322.